MW00653151

CRAPPY FRIENDS

THE GUIDE TO FEMALE FRIENDSHIPS: THE GOOD, THE BAD, THE UGLY

KRISTAN HIGGINS
JOSS DEY

CRAPPY FRIENDS

The Ultimate Guide to Female Friendship:

The Good, The Bad, The Ugly

www.crappyfriends.com

Cover photo: Jennifer Turner

Edited by: Deborah Cannarella

ISBN: 978-0-578-77812-9

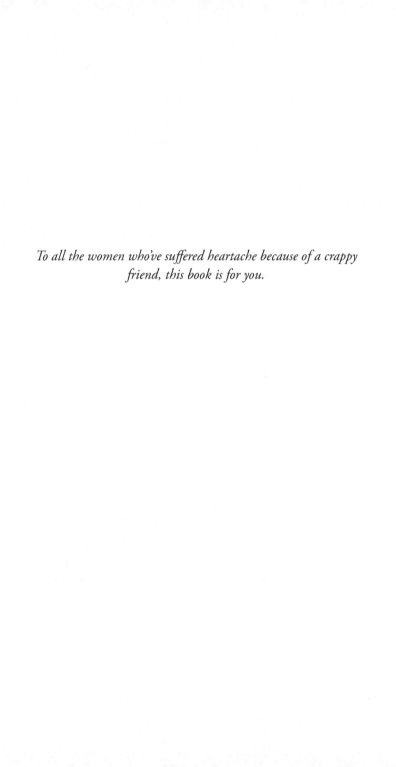

To all the women who've suffered heartache because of a crappy friend, this book is for you.

ACKNOWLEDGMENTS

We would like to acknowledge that we did next to nothing to make this podcast, and this book, anything other than what it is—two friends talking about friendship, hoping to help women who've agonized over what went wrong the same way we have. *Organic* is one word to describe our efforts; disorganized, last minute, haphazard are others. But man, we've had fun.

Thanks to Dr. Khaleesi, fake name of our real-life friend and board-certified practicing psychologist, who has helped us with some of the more difficult issues in our podcast. Thanks to Jennifer Iszkiewicz, our amazing pal and purveyor of the best food and biggest laughs. To the Princess, Kristan's daughter (and Joss's would-be daughter), who chimes in from time to time. Thanks to Anne Renwick for her help and advice on book production; Jennifer Turner for our smashing cover and promotional photos; Deborah Cannarella for copyediting; Madison Terrill for her research.

To our dozens—nay, hundreds, perhaps even *thousands*—of listeners to the podcast, thank you so much! We adore you.

And thanks to you, readers. We wish you nothing but the best.

For more information on Crappy Friends, visit www.crappyfriends.net. You can find Kristan at www.kristanhiggins.com and Joss at www.jossdey.com.

CONTENTS

PREFACE

Dear Reader,

If you're reading this, you've probably had a crappy friend.

So have we.

So have most women.

The two of us, Joss and Kristan—aka the Ladies—have been friends for more than fifteen years. We have a shared love of writing and thoughtfully made cocktails, dogs and eating out. But what made us jump the fence to a deeper and more trusting friendship? To that place where we could tell each other anything, no matter how dark?

It was a single conversation. One day, tentative and unsure, we both confessed that we'd had a…well, hell, the words are still hard to get out…a crappy friend.

Female friendship is supposed to be sacred. Movies like *Thelma and Louise*, *Steel Magnolias*, *Bridesmaids* and *Girls Night* tell us that good people have good friends forever. To the grave. You meet in kindergarten, middle school or high school. In college or at your first job or in Lamaze class. Your kids become playmates, and you become besties. It's not supposed to end ever—let alone end badly.

But here we were, both admitting that our hearts had been broken, and not by romance but by something even more baffling. By a close friendship, maybe by our *best-friend* friendship.

Our experiences were devastating. Neither of us knew how to process them. We were both ashamed of our inability to maintain something that, according to friendship lore, should have lasted all our lives. What did it say about us that we'd once loved these women, cherished our friendships, and then decided to never speak with them again? What was wrong with us? Were we monsters, lacking in a fundamental goodness? Were we cold-hearted and unlovable? Were we dumb? Did we lack good judgment?

Honestly, we didn't know. No one talks about this stuff.

When we finally told each other our different (yet so similar) stories, the relief was immeasurable. We were no longer *alone*. Someone else had experienced that silent devastation.

Sometimes, the death of a friendship can hurt *more* than a romantic breakup. The expectation for women to stay friends forever—to have a special bond, to be soul sisters or sisters of the heart—is everywhere and, so often, completely unrealistic. But none of us have to put up with crappy friends.

This book will outline certain themes and issues that crop up in many a female friendship. You'll probably find yourself nodding along, saying, "Yep, been there!" We'll also give you guidelines on how to vet friends, really get to know them, keep appropriate boundaries, learn to get closer. We'll walk you through how to break up with a friend when you have to…and how to grieve and move on from a friendship when you're the one being dumped.

The motto of our Crappy Friends podcast is "Girl power defeating bitchery." Don't get us wrong. A true friend is worth her weight in rubies. But every friendship is imperfect, just as every human is imperfect. Our podcast and this book are intended to help you:

- give yourself permission to ditch a truly crappy friend;
- stop viewing time spent with a crappy friend as punishment or community service;
- include friendship as part of your self-care regime; and
- make room for more positivity in your life.

We hope you to give you the tools you need to think clearly about your relationships, communicate with honesty and compassion and make the type of friendships that make your life shine.

We're so glad you're here!

Kristan and Joss

CHAPTER 1

STUCK IN A CRAPPY FRIENDSHIP?

MAYBE YOU'RE READING THIS BECAUSE:

1. you're looking but can't seem to find that mythical sister-from-another-mister best friend;
2. you're in a friendship with a person you're not sure you even like, yet for some reason are giving that person way too much head space and time;
3. you've been dumped by someone you adored and are gobsmacked but pretending you're *fine*, just fine;
4. all of the above.

For many women, friendship can have a more powerful role in life than a relationship with a romantic partner, family member or career. We invest time, energy and emotions in our friendships, nurture them, think about them, and sometimes agonize over them.

In prehistoric days, women were the caretakers and child raisers; as we evolved, we learned to brew coffee and make hors d'oeuvres while the hunters and gatherers were out killing woolly mammoths. Only in recent generations have women started taking on the same jobs as men. But for generations, for *millenia*, women have gathered together and gotten shit done. Bonding, making friends and being friends forever feels like part of our evolutionary makeup.

There has been plenty of evidence throughout time of women working together, supporting each other, bonding. *Crappy* friends, though—where are they discussed in the history books? Are there cave drawings of women clubbing each other around the fire? No. Instead, we're given Celie, Shug and Nettie in *The Color Purple.* Jane and Helen in *Jane Eyre.* Anne and Diana in *Anne of Green Gables.* Everyone in *Steel Magnolias.* When there *is* a wretched female friendship in the movies, someone ends up dead (not an option we recommend).

These storybook friendships are why the idea of *friends till the end* is a tough one to shake. Every woman we know—including each of us—has had a friend she'd like to ditch but just can't. Instead, we let that person eat up time in our lives and space in our heads. The imaginary conversations we have! The text messages and emails we don't send! The times we've bitten our tongues so hard they bleed!

Why?

Why do we tolerate the situation? Would we put up with a romantic partner who made us feel this way? Hopefully not. But, we tell ourselves, we have *history* with our friends. There have been some good times. They knew us when. And this idea of ending a friendship can be terrifying and traumatic. Sucking it up, accepting that you're wasting your time, enduring the crappiest pal, can be easier than what Kristan calls the "special friendship unicorn"—that one difficult, honest conversation.

Whether you're the friend someone wants to dump or the friend who wants to shake someone loose, that conversation can be ridiculously hard to have. Too many times, we stay in a crappy friendship just out of habit or fear.

You've known Narcissa (not her real name) since *kindergarten*. Yes, she's a self-absorbed pain in the ass who never takes the time to ask about you, but she's *your* pain in the ass. Then, little by little, you realize that every time you talk to her, see her, text her, you feel worse. Are you obliged to include her in your life forever? Do the ties that start in kindergarten condemn you to years of miserable, one-sided encounters with Narcissa?

Breaking up, as the song tells us, is hard to do. We don't want to sound *mean*. We don't want to make Narcissa uncomfortable. A lot of us women are trained from birth to be *nice*, even when that means sacrificing our own comfort and going against what we know is right. "It's fine," we say instead. "I can put up with it. After all, she's my *friend*. We've known each other all these years."

And so, we suck up *decades* of a mediocre or downright shitty friendship, suffering through it but still not doing anything about it.

Girlfriend, you deserve better. We're gonna help you get it.

CHAPTER 2

THE USER: JOSS'S STORY

BY THE TIME I REALIZED MY FRIEND WAS A USER, I HAD cleaned out my savings and uprooted my life. Actually, I didn't fully realize my friend was a user until long after I'd been dumped and discarded. In fact, I struggled with the humiliation and bewilderment of being dumped for years before I understood how calculated and systematic my friend's behavior had been from the very start.

As you might imagine, my friend, Euphemia (not her real name) and I started off as Insta-Friends. This type of friendship usually has six stages:

Stage 1: Your eyes meet across a crowded room (or in a Facebook group). You grin at each other because the snark sparkling in her eyes matches the snark twinkling in yours.
Stage 2: A few conversations make you think, "We have so much in common, it's like we're sisters!"
Stage 3: You decide to do everything together!
Stage 4: You see something a little off, but *don't* say something.

And then, in cases involving a User:

Stage 5: You realize that the friendship is a one-way street, and traffic always flows from you to her.
Stage 6: You discover that you are no longer useful.

Although Euphemia and I met online, our friendship followed the Insta-Friendship stages exactly. For me, the immediate connection validated our friendship, despite behaviors that made me uneasy. I told myself, "This kind of thing doesn't happen every day, which means it's the real deal, which means we are best friends forever!" I really believed that.

The "True" Confidante

Euphemia and I are both writers. When we met, I was a newbie, and she had been published. I read one of her books, loved it and sent her a fan letter. We became email buddies, occasionally speaking on the phone.

At the beginning of our friendship I was too insecure about my writing to admit to Euphemia that I wanted to be a published writer, too, but she guessed it based on our correspondence. "I knew it!" she crowed when I finally confirmed her suspicions. She was so supportive and excited, making me feel like my talent was the buried treasure she'd searched hard to find. She made me feel *seen*.

Euphemia was bold, charismatic, confident and hilarious, especially about her past relationships—the opposite of me. But opposites attract, right? She'd been married a few times, and every story she told about her exes was funnier than the last. Not self-deprecating funny, but mean, cutting and, oftentimes, cruel-funny.

Have you ever done that thing where you laugh at something someone's says even though you know you shouldn't? You're shocked at first, but then you chuckle along with your friend. You think, *oh she's so bad!* as you laugh and laugh, enchanted that she's letting you see this side of her. There's trust there…she's telling you something she wouldn't tell anyone else (or so you think). Intimacy grows, and you feel privileged that this bright creature is letting you see this side of her. Euphemia trusted me with her secrets, which made me feel special. She didn't just see me as a talented writer, but, I thought, as a true confidante.

Those types of exchanges happened many times with Euphemia. Each time she revealed some scandalous thing about one of her exes (*he has such a* small *problem*) or even about herself (*sonuvabitch gave me crabs a month after we were married!*), I thought we were getting closer because I knew things *no one else* knew about her. She trusted me with her secrets.

Looking back now, I see how one-dimensional her representations of her partners were. To hear her tell it, they were all losers who couldn't appreciate how *amazing* she was. She never took responsibility for her part in the demise of any of those relationships

Her: Rockstar. You: Groupie

The rockstar friend is not looking for an equal. She wants you to stay in your place, beneath her in life. That way, she can maintain her sense of superiority, making it seem like she's Yoda to your Luke Skywalker *and* also your best friend. But you don't know all this in the beginning.

My life on the East Coast had stalled. I had a shitty job, and sure, I had an MFA in creative writing, but I still didn't really know how to write books. Euphemia, on the other hand, lived in a midwestern state she made sound *amazing*.

At her invitation, I visited, more than once, and we had the best times. Booze-filled evenings filled with raucous laughter and rich food. Our bond deepened over mimosas, all-you-can-eat brunch buffets and *Buffy the Vampire Slayer* marathons.

It was Euphemia's idea for me to move to her city. How great it would be! I'd find a job instantly, she proclaimed, *and* we could help each other with our writing. How flattering! How thrilling! I thought, "Why not? I'm young! It would be a blast to live in another part of the country, especially this fabulous midwestern state, with my *best friend*."

So I quit my job, packed my car, and drove.

I did find a job almost immediately. I got a cute apartment. Things were going great. I was getting to know the fabulous midwestern state, and Euphemia was there. We talked and hung out all the time. She introduced me to her other friends, the women she had occasional drinks or dinner with. I met her writer friends, some of whom had also been published, and they were welcoming and generous with their knowledge.

Being a writer was always my dream, and Euphemia presented herself as the architect of seeing that become a reality. I was excited, grateful and felt *so, so lucky* that I met Euphemia. I felt honored that this amazing writer liked me at all. We were true BFFs, I thought. In reality, I was a puppy, and she was basking in my adoration.

Euphemia asked me to help her plot and beta-read her books. I was thrilled and happy to do it. She was the more successful writer, with an agent and editors at a big publishing house, and I was just a newbie. "She must really value me to ask for my opinion," I thought. We were partners! She would help me with my writing, too!

Except she didn't. Even though she offered, she never had time to listen to my book ideas or read my pages. I asked for her help; she never had time. I excused her, assuming that she was busy with her day job and her writing career, which was starting to blow up. Of course she was *busy*. I was her *best friend*, so I let it go.

By this point in our relationship, I trusted her implicitly, listing her as my emergency contact at work and with my landlord. I instructed my parents to call her if they couldn't reach me for any reason. She was family to me, speaking a secret language of shared looks, finishing each other's sentences and having a shared intuition that I thought only siblings experienced.

How *Dare* You Have Your Own Life?

Three months into my new job in the fabulous midwestern state, it came to light that my boss was embezzling money from the company. Our local office would be shut down.

I started interviewing for new jobs right away and tried to remain positive, but I was terrified. I have a chronic disease and desperately need healthcare even more than most people. Missing my medication literally meant that in a month or so, I might wake up and be unable to walk. Until I found a new job, I would have to choose between paying for medication or for other things—like food and rent. I was frantic to find a new job that provided healthcare benefits: the wretched dilemma of an American with a chronic illness. A month after I'd been laid off, my insurance ran out. I could not afford any of the available plans. Unable to take my meds, I started to feel like shit. But, I thought, at least I had my best friend there for me. Right?

Wrong.

Euphemia didn't seem too concerned about my situation. I'm sure I leaned on her emotionally. Of course I did! She was my *best friend*. I sensed no change in our relationship. No disturbance in the Force, as it were. Even with my fears about my livelihood and health, I made a point of remaining cheerful around her, not wanting to be a little black raincloud.

Eight weeks after I was laid off, and a month without medication, I got a job offer. I accepted it immediately. First thing I did was to sort out my insurance and get my meds. Finally, things were looking up, and I was on the mend. Finally, I could regain my footing, focus on writing in my free time and continue to put roots down in the fabulous midwestern state.

And then Euphemia stopped communicating with me. She just stopped. One day we were talking, the next day, nothing. No emails. No returned phone calls. I was utterly bewildered and even worried that something was dreadfully wrong. I went to her house to find out. When I asked her what was going on, she said that I was "down and depressed all the time." She said I was a "drain to be around." She said she couldn't be "the beginning and end for me," whatever the hell that meant. Suddenly, I was *persona non grata*. Euphemia ended her tirade by suggesting I go back home. It had been exactly six months since I moved to the fabulous midwestern state.

I was *devastated*. I couldn't speak. Sitting there in her house, where we'd had so many fun times, I felt the tears pouring out of my eyes. I had just enough pride left that I didn't want her to see me sob, so I just nodded. I left her house and never spoke to her again. She had made herself abundantly clear. Our "friendship" was dead.

All but one of her friends stopped talking to me too. Euphemia had always been the queen bee of the group, so, in retrospect, this wasn't a huge surprise, but at the time, it was shocking. What story did she tell them to convince them that I deserved this rejection? I'd been *so careful* not to be a burden to anyone, even when my pain levels were skyrocketing. I never once asked for help, a loan or a job lead. What had she told them? My insecurity, usually at manageable levels, suddenly metastasized.

So yeah, I got dumped, and it broke me in ways I never could have imagined and had never experienced before. But I hid my feelings. I told no one because I was deeply ashamed. How could I have let this happen? How could I have missed all those red flags? Why did I trust this person who only pretended to like me? And later I wondered, how could I let it affect me so deeply? She was only a *friend*, after all. Why was it taking so long for me to get over this?

A few months after the dumping, I went for a routine gynecological exam. My pap smear came back abnormal. There was a higher-than-normal reading on a test that can sometimes indicate cancer.

Cancer.

Yeah. Holy shit.

My doctor questioned me about what was going on in my life. She said that we would watch things but she suspected that the irregularity was stress-related.

"Have you experienced a death or divorce?" she asked.

"No, god no." Then, irrationally embarrassed, not sure that what I was about to reveal even counted, grateful for doctor-patient confidentiality, I added, "Well, my best friend just dumped me."

"Yes, yes. That makes sense," she said clinically, making a notation on her clipboard.

I was *shocked*. It never occurred to me that my friendships could have such a profound effect on my physical being. It never occurred to me that a medical professional would deem a broken friendship to be an important factor in my health. I mean, the death of someone close is a huge, traumatic thing. So is divorce. But friendship?

Yes.

The loss of friendship is a real trauma, as real as a death or divorce. And why shouldn't it be? We make space in our lives for our friends. We give them our hearts. Their losses become ours, and so do their successes. The demise of a friendship is worthy of your grief, dear readers. Remember that.

The Aftermath

After a few months, I took Euphemia's callous advice and went back home. I had been living thousands of miles away from friends, family and any familiar resource. I was as alone geographically and emotionally as I've ever been, and I needed to be around people who genuinely cared for me. I wanted my mom and dad, a fact that galled the hell out of me. I was in my mid-thirties, for crying out loud.

To summarize: I felt stupid for putting my trust so completely in someone so unworthy. I was ashamed that I couldn't make life work in a new place. I'd failed at the most basic thing in the world: having a good friend.

Shame is a very powerful thing. It is an amorphous, immovable burden. The shame of what happened paralyzed me. I became extremely cautious when it came to making new friends—and not in the positive way we talk about later in this book. My scars were brand new, too deep and hadn't begun to scab over yet. I was pleasant to people, but there was an "Authorized Personnel Only" sign on my forehead. If you were someone new, you were not authorized.

I did not authorize anyone for a very long time. There were lessons to be learned. Many lessons:

- People who talk trash about their loved ones will talk trash about anyone. You aren't immune. It just isn't your turn yet.
- You deserve friends who reciprocate your friendship.
- If your friend is not supportive when you're going through a rough patch, she is no friend at all.

Eventually, as chance would have it, and despite all my hesitancy, I did make a friend. Another successful writer, if you can believe it. She was kind right from the start, respecting the imaginary sign on my head until I finally took it down. The differences between this woman and Euphemia are stark:

- Even though she *is* a star, she makes me feel like we are the same—just regular people. Hilarious, kind, quirky, flawed regular people who like to write about people like us.
- She offers to help me with my writing and then actually helps me with my writing.
- She shows up. If I am confused or troubled or in pain, she sees right through all my stoic efforts to hide that and shows up.

So, years later, I finally told this new friend my secret— I'd been dumped—and then she told me hers. Many secrets later, we started a podcast called *Crappy Friends* and wrote this book together.

THE USER: LESSONS FROM THE TRENCHES

Stage 1: Your eyes meet across a crowded room (or in a Facebook group). You grin at each other because the snark sparkling in her eyes matches the snark twinkling in yours.

Stage 2: A few conversations make you think, "We have so much in common, it's like we're sisters!"

Stage 3: You decide to do everything together!

Stage 4: You see something a little off, but *don't* say something.

Stage 5: You realize that the friendship is a one-way street, and traffic always flows from you to her.

Stage 6: You discover that you are no longer useful.

CHAPTER 3

INSTA-FRIENDS: KRISTAN'S STORY

INSTA-FRIENDSHIP, NOUN.

The false assumption that you can know a person inside and out in a short period of time, usually precipitated by "hitting it off" at an initial meeting

So many of the letters from our podcast listeners are about this very phenomenon. If you've had trouble with an Insta-Friend, as Joss detailed in the previous chapter, you are not alone.

I've been there, too, more than once and twice with heartbreaking dismay when all I thought to be true was false. One insta-friend was a user, as with Joss's story. The other was just a hot mess of confusion and anger

The problem with an Insta-Friendship is that the joy and connection you feel seems so *real*. So fun! What could be more exhilarating than meeting a person you want to talk to for hours? A friend who laughs at your jokes and is so perfect for you! It's thrilling.

It's also false.

Don't get me wrong. When you meet some people, you think, "Yes, this person and I are destined to be great friends." And you may be right! How fantastic if you are! But listen to your Auntie Kristan. I have a story to tell you.

I met my first Insta-Friend at a writers conference. Like me, she didn't know too many people. We bonded immediately—she had a bright smile and sparkly eyes, and we hit it off. We had so much in common! It was crazy!

Insta-Friend Fact: There are people out there who will lie, obfuscate or stretch the truth to seem like they have more in common with you than they actually do. They may not be aware that they're doing this, but take all those "Oh, my God! Me too!" exclamations with a grain of salt.

But I was naïve back then. Gloriana (not her real name) and I seemed to have an *uncanny* number of things in common. We were both happily married, devoted moms of young children, loved to read, loved to write. We made each other laugh, admitted our insecurities about attending this big conference, shared our love of the same authors. We had *so* much fun that night. I felt like I had made a new best friend.

Insta-Friend Fact: You cannot make a best friend in one evening.

Again, I was a rube back then. Gloriana was one of the few people I knew at the conference. In that big, noisy hotel full of famous authors, it was fantastic to have a buddy.

Gloriana was amazingly energetic and accomplished in my eyes. She had lived all over the country, had served in the military, held down a challenging and stimulating full-time job while also writing and somehow homeschooling her kids! Wow, right? (Um …no, not right. More later).

I took Gloriana at face value and accepted everything she said. I mean, why wouldn't I? It's not my nature to be suspicious, to wonder if a stranger is lying to my face. We lived in different parts of the country, so we never saw each other in the day-to-day reality of life. A grain of salt comes in handy when you hear a long list of amazing and unbelievable accomplishments—a lesson I'd have to learn more than once, alas.

After the conference, Gloriana and I stayed in close touch through email. One day, she said she had a hankering to visit New York City, which is not far from my home. She was planning to take the train in. Would I meet her in the city?

I sure would! We met for a day of strolling, eating and Christmas shopping. The stories and laughter flowed. Compared to my stable, happy and pleasantly drama-free life, hers seemed so colorful and wild. I loved hearing her stories.

We roomed together at another conference. We went away for a plotting weekend with a couple of other authors, and our friendship strengthened. When I had a speaking gig in her state, I invited her to crash in my hotel for the duration.

However …a few red flags started to rise up. Gloriana talked a lot about ex-best friends who had done her wrong. A lot—I mean, a *lot*—of relatives had been absolutely horrible to her. The poor thing, I thought! How could anyone not adore this woman? But a pattern was emerging—Gloriana as steadfast and devoted, other people as callous and self-absorbed. "Man!" I thought. "She sure has crap luck in the friend department! Lucky she has me now!"

**Insta-Friend Fact: When a friend tells you stories about
The Many Horrible People Who Didn't Appreciate Her,
pay attention. You'll be the next story.**

A second red flag was her grandiosity. It took me a while to
recognize that one, because, again, I never interacted with
Gloriana in her everyday life—and I was naïve and trusting.
So when she told me that one of her kids wanted to attend a
very prestigious New England university not far from me, I
was thrilled. The college was recruiting Baby Girl hard,
Gloriana said, since her child was genius-level smart. Wow! I
was so excited. I could be like an aunt to this kid, cook her
dinner, let her do laundry at my house, go to college events
—it would be great! Gloriana said she was grateful and happy
that her kid would have "family" nearby. It did feel that way
…like we were family.

They never visited the hallowed halls. I asked a few times
when the college tour would be, inviting Gloriana and her
family to stay at our house for a long weekend, but she
always dodged committing to a date. Weird, when one of the
most prestigious schools in the *world* is recruiting your kid,
but …whatever. The subject of university was dropped, and
Baby Girl stopped coming up in conversation.

Not long after, Gloriana told me her son was going to
become a member of an incredibly elite group of the military.
She knew this because he, a high school junior, was already
training with them. "How does that work?" I asked. "They
just let a kid work out with them? They let him come on the
base without clearance?" Yes, she said. They did.

It sounded a bit far-fetched, even to my civilian mind.
Later, I would learn that this particular military group
trained three thousand miles away from where Gloriana and
her family then lived.

Gloriana's job, which she had described as corporate

trainer, turned out to be head server in a chain restaurant. Now all the times she'd dodged my questions on what a corporate trainer actually *was* made sense. But why? I was the queen of blue-collar jobs: typist, nanny, waitress, hotel maid, house cleaner. There was no shame in hard work—not to me. So why didn't Gloriana just tell the truth and say she trained the wait staff at a local chain restaurant? Why pitch it as a mysterious and powerful corporate job for months and months?

Insta-Friend Fact: If things in your friend's life seem to be too good to be true, they probably are.

When a person makes grandiose, sometimes outrageous false claims, it's because she doesn't feel her real life is enough. Ivy League schools, Special Forces, exaggerated job titles…insecurity, you old bastard. Stop messing with people.

In the movie *Romy and Michelle's High School Reunion*, the lead characters tell their former classmates they invented sticky notes, a claim quickly disproved. That's how Gloriana's stories started to sound. I stopped believing her hyperbole. I tried to let her know that she didn't have to exaggerate for me to like her. My Achilles heel is dishonesty. Lots of writers exaggerate, but *everything* in Gloriana's life seemed so big, so extraordinary, so dramatic that it became hard to believe anything about it.

Our love of writing, which had brought us together, now was becoming a cause for division. My career was taking off; she never got off the ground, switching from book idea to book idea, unable to see a project through, even when she had interest from a big publisher. I don't think it was jealousy —not at all—but I started to see her anger when we got together. Not a new anger, but something I hadn't seen at first, or hadn't wanted to see. It had been a few years since those first happy get-togethers. Now, Gloriana wanted to day-drink (another red flag was how much she loved to drink) and talk about old flames or her dramatic fights with her husband.

I began losing patience. I had *loved* those book talks, those plotting sessions, and I had loved the more cheerful, optimistic Gloriana. But the more I learned about her life, the more I realized those images were false.

Did I talk to her about that? Nope. I was a coward. You see, because of those first couple of wonderful weekends together, I kept hoping to find the old Gloriana again. The Insta-Friend Gloriana. And, I admit shamefully, I was afraid of incurring her wrath. Gloriana was always mad at *someone*, and many of her stories were about how Friend X or Aunt Y had wronged her. Someone was always stabbing her in the back, letting her down, breaking her heart, taking advantage of her. She would talk about these people for *hours* without stopping. My role was to be her rapt audience.

I grew up with a sibling who was always angry and unpredictable. It was horrible. As a result, I shy away from anger. It takes a lot for me to deal with someone who is furious, yelling, fuming. So I said nothing. I didn't want to stir the pot. Gloriana and I only saw each other a couple of times a year, so I could tolerate it. Right?

Insta-Friend Fact: When you find yourself not wanting to spend time with your Insta-Friend, it's time to take a closer look.

In the beginning of our Insta-Friendship, Gloriana and I had laughed until it hurt. Not anymore. I didn't want to see her as much as I once had, but I clung to the hope that we'd click back in, and the "original" Gloriana would return.

Insta-Friend Fact: The "original" version of your Insta-Friend is often an illusion.

Eventually, inevitably, Gloriana's anger turned on me. I had to cancel a trip to meet her in the city. Why? Well, I'd had a bad fall that required surgery, and my surgeon had to reschedule because of a difficult pregnancy. Hence, I wouldn't be able to walk on our chosen date, not without burning pain and crutches. I told her we'd have to put the trip off until a good six weeks after my surgery.

Gloriana did *not* like that. Not one bit. I was baffled—she did realize I couldn't walk, right? She told me she needed to see me in person—we lived eight hours apart—and said that sometimes, a friend should make the effort, even if just to meet for coffee.

That idea struck me as ridiculous. I was writing full-time and had two school-age kids. I was managing their myriad activities, my marriage, family obligations and this new career of mine. Making a 16-hour round trip drive because she wanted a face-to-face *now*? I couldn't do it. (And honestly, I didn't want to.) I didn't have the time or inclination to drive or take the train to see her. I couldn't afford it, either. Discretionary income was scarce during those years.

We didn't talk for a while. We weren't officially not speaking, but our friendship was getting really complicated. It wasn't fun anymore. My hope of finding that original version of Gloriana was dead, and I realized she had never really existed. The upbeat, positive, cheerful mom and aspiring writer I had first met was not the whole person. And the aching, horrible truth was, I didn't like the whole person. I wanted to, but I didn't trust her, and I shied away from her anger and resentment

The tension between us came to a head after a tiny, seemingly meaningless exchange. She'd taken offense at something

I'd posted online about Facebook, of all things—I'd said that I wished the powers-that-be would stop changing how things looked, because it was hard to relearn the site every four days. That was it.

And suddenly, there in my comments, was a diatribe from Gloriana about how *ungrateful* I was…to Facebook. After all, she wrote, the site was free to use! How dare I question its makers! (Funny, how time gives you perspective on things, isn't it?) Because I felt like she was picking a fight, and because her hostility felt so displaced, so public and so *strange*,

I deleted her over-the-top comments (I am a public person, after all, and don't like anger to be on my pages). And then I sent her an email.

Are you mad at me? I asked in an email. *About Facebook?*

She told me our friendship had problems. That while she loved me fiercely, she needed *more* from me. The fact that I had canceled the New York City trip was profoundly upsetting to her, and my reason (my torn-up leg) wasn't acceptable. She was my soul sister, she said, and she was *owed* her a certain amount of my time and energy. Wasn't her need to see me then just as important as it would be if she lay dying in the hospital? (My answer: No.) To save our friendship, she explained, we would have to "go through this storm together and emerge stronger." Picking apart our friendship would be hard, she said, and we would have scars that would last a lifetime, but it would be worth it.

My initial reaction when I learned of the level of her feelings, her anger and distress was to jump in and fix things. I'm Catholic. Accepting blame is part of who I am. HOW could I have been so terrible, so thoughtless? My fear of angry people reared up, and, at first, I said I'd do anything she needed to save our friendship. (I wish I could go back in time and slap myself for that.)

I was all set to gird my loins for the storm of saving our friendship…and then I stepped back and took a breath.

Gloriana had said I was hugely important in her life—which I thought was odd, because we almost *never* talked on the phone, and in five years had seen each other a handful of times. Aside from the first couple of times, it hadn't been great. Gloriana's outpouring of anger and hurt…it seemed out of proportion for the friendship we actually had. In my heart, I knew Gloriana *wasn't* a top priority in my life.

Gloriana and I had had a lot of fun in those Insta-Friendship days. We'd had a great honeymoon, but the marriage part of our friendship was utter crap. For *years* I had been telling myself she was a good friend whose company I loved, and for years I'd been lying to myself. I reminded myself that friendships, of all the relationships in life, should be enjoyable. You can't pick your family, but you get to pick your friends …and this friend was exhausting. She was smart, funny, up for anything, but she was also angry, righteous, needy and self-centered

I emailed her back and, in what I thought was as gentle a way as possible, thanked her for the five years of friendship. I wrote:

I think you need more from our friendship than I can or want to give. I've always enjoyed our times together—very much—but the thought of going through storms and emerging scarred and wounded after purging and venting and examining …it just made me feel weary. After reading about how strongly you felt, and how long you'd felt so many negative emotions, I just didn't see how I could feel the same way about our friendship. I think I'd always be waiting for the other shoe to drop

See, the thing is, I have a *lot* of good friends. I've *always* had close friends: Beth who grew up next door to me,

Catherine from freshman year of college, Brian from Holy Cross, Heidi from my first job, JoAnn from my last job. I also *keep* most of my friends, which didn't seem like a pattern for Gloriana, not with all the stories of betrayal she'd told me. Not *one* of my other friends had ever made so many demands on me or had so many problems with me as Gloriana did.

I ended my email by wishing her and her lovely family the very, very best.

As soon as I hit send, I felt relieved. I had handled the situation, finally, in what I thought was a mature and kind-hearted way. It had not been easy to write those things, and it made me feel sick to know she was hurt. But our friendship had come to its obvious conclusion.

She was angry. No, she was furious. She hadn't seen a breakup as a possibility, and she posted vague, angry things about friendship for awhile. I didn't respond. I hated that I hurt her, I really did. But mostly, I was relieved.

Our paths no longer cross, although I have donated a few times to a foundation she works for, and she thanked me warmly for it. We have a few mutual acquaintances. One of her kids reposted something of mine a while back and called me her "auntie." That made me smile. I like to think that if Gloriana and I ran into each other now, we'd have a nice chat, both of us older and wiser now.

Insta-Friend Fact: Real friendship takes time.

I was so thrilled with the idea of finding a new bestie at the age of forty-one that I didn't look more closely. Had I taken time, paid attention to recurring patterns, I think Gloriana and I might have become friendly acquaintances, not "soul sisters" who later had to break up, which hurt us both.

I really loved parts of Gloriana, in all her messiness and spin. She was fascinating and intelligent, but as time went on, I realized I wasn't *comfortable* with her. And if you're not comfortable with a friend, is she truly a friend? Gloriana and I were both seduced by the idea of that magical connection, that initial sparkliness we felt. It's a theme has echoed in many, many letters from listeners to our podcast. *We were so close at first! I had never felt that connection with any friend before! I just want to go back to how things were before.*

But you can't go back. With Insta-Friends, the "before" isn't real. You *weren't* ever that close. You made assumptions, and many of them turned out to be false. The tingly connection is the same you might feel when seeing a gorgeous stranger. A tingle is not the same as true love. Can it grow into that? Sure! But true love, romantic or otherwise, takes time.

My friendship with Gloriana was not meant to last, no matter how sparkly it seemed at first. And that's okay.

The lesson here, and one we've talked about so often on our show, is that the instant best friend is a myth. Your initial response to a person might turn out to be right on the money, but only time will tell.

INSTA-FRIENDS: LESSONS FROM THE TRENCHES

1. There are people out there who will lie, obfuscate or stretch the truth to seem like they have more in common with you than they actually do.
2. You cannot make a best friend in one evening.
3. When a friend tells you stories about The Many Horrible People Who Didn't Appreciate Her, pay attention. You'll be in the next story.

4. If things in your friend's life seem too good to be true, they probably aren't.
5. When you find yourself not wanting to spend time with your Insta-Friend, it's time to call it quits.
6. The "original" version of your Insta-Friend never returns.
7. Real friendship takes time.

CHAPTER 4

DRAPED IN RED FLAGS

THIS IS THE STORY OF HOW WE LADIES BECAME SUPER-close friends during our struggle with a mutual friend. The resulting turmoil is one of the reasons we started our podcast. We had to look long and hard at what makes a friendship work—and what breaks one.

We had to ask ourselves: *Why didn't we lay down some ground rules? Why didn't we address problems as they arose? Why didn't we get out sooner?*

Because it's hard to do those things. It's hard to tell someone who considers you a friend that she's gone too far. That you know she's lying. That you don't feel comfortable listening to her talk about certain subjects. That you don't share the same values, which is, for you, a fundamental problem that cannot be overcome.

We should have tried anyway, but we took the easy path instead—and, man, did it get ugly.

This is the story of our friend Iphigenia (not her real name) and how our friendship:

- started off on seemingly firm ground;

- veered off course;
- how we tried to salvage it;
- and what happened in the aftermath.

We failed Iphigenia—make no mistake. If we'd spoken up earlier, been more forthright, maybe things would've been different. Probably not, but maybe. Maybe Iphigenia then would've understood what kind of response her actions created and tried to be more sensitive. Maybe we would have gotten out earlier and not allowed her to feel so close to us.

We were the crappy friends. So was she, but we did not handle things well.

It's good to note here that Iphigenia has moved to another part of the country and seems to be doing well, and we truly wish her the very best.

As you read this, you might think, "My God, Ladies, you are incredibly dumb!" And we are. Rather, we *were*. But keep in mind that all these experiences unfolded over *years* of friendship. The red flags were there, and by the end, yes, Iphigenia wasn't even hiding them. But we didn't *want* to see them. We ducked and dodged and rationalized. We *wanted* to like Iphy! She was a writer, like us. She was energetic and cheerful, enthusiastic to work on her book, like us. And we were her only female friends.

Red Flag #1: She doesn't have other female friends.

Listen. We love our male friends. But based on our experiences, women who don't have female friends—who announce that fact as a badge of honor—are warning you away. Listen to them! "I get along better with men," they might say, or, "It's just easier to talk to men. They're so straightforward. No drama."

Maybe she frames it as shyness or believes that most

women don't care enough to get to know her. Maybe she says, "I was burned by a female friend in the past"—the victim approach, discussed in a later chapter.

When a woman tells you up front that she doesn't have women friends, she's hoping that you will rise to the challenge and befriend her. That you will do *all the work* to prove that your entire gender is worthy. This is a ridiculous, unwinnable task.

But you don't know this (we didn't). Instead, you think, *Wow, I must be very special, since no other woman has passed muster! Now that I think of it, I* am *pretty great.*

You're not. We were not. We were just the latest women to fail with Iphy.

Iphy didn't have female friends because, according to her, she hated the innate, inescapable female drama. According to Iphigenia, women were the *worst* (Hey! Misogyny, anyone? Or irony?—keep reading). Plus, men *liked* her. They were easier to get along with and simpler, as Iphy herself professed to be.

When Iphy showed up at our writers' group, we welcomed her in. She was hesitant, given her aforementioned ideas about the female penchant for drama, competitiveness, mean-girl-ness (neither of us Ladies had experienced that behavior in this group at all). Iphy soon said she didn't like most of the women. Just us.

Huh? Well, okay, then. Odd, but sort of …flattering? Within a few weeks, we'd formed a little foursome—Iphy, Joss, Kristan and a third friend, Sharon (not her real name). We had laughs, mutual interests and some commonalities, and we looked forward to seeing each other. We also formed a writers' critique group that met weekly, minus Kristan.

Red Flag #2: She asks for help and advice and then refuses to take it.

From the start, things did not go well in the critique group. We noticed that although Iphy asked for our input, she never changed a word. When the four of us went away for weekend writing retreats, one of us would make a suggestion, only to have Iphigenia spend an hour telling us why her initial choice was correct. She always claimed to know someone who had done *exactly* what her character had done, so her story was fine as it was.

It was her call, of course, but why ask for input if she really didn't want any? The point of these weekends was to get everyone's feedback so the writer could fill in the holes and work on the problems. Two of us were published, one had finished a manuscript…and Iphy was unable to finish a story. She had never been published, and she wasn't getting good feedback from industry professionals. She was often told her work was overly dramatic and unbelievable, but she dismissed that feedback, too.

Iphigenia seemed both insecure and grandiose. She once had different goals, but a bout with cancer had derailed them, and she hadn't been able to follow through. Now that she was healthy, she told us, she wanted to return to her original field—teaching—and we encouraged her to do so.

By her own admission, Iphy was underemployed. In her job, she sat for long stretches of time, waiting to be needed. When she *was* called on to work, her work was brief and physical. In her own words, it was "brainless" and a "way to fill the time." What she *really* wanted to do was write novels on the side while teaching art.

But if we asked about teaching jobs, or state certification, she'd suddenly change tunes, saying she was *so* happy at her job, which she now defended as being heroic and exciting.

We didn't know what to believe—was she bored, or stimulated? Did she want to be a teacher, or stay at her job? Did she really want to be published, or was she writing for fun? The answers varied greatly, and it became harder and harder to be encouraging, since her answers changed with the wind.

Red Flag #3: No one else shows up for her.

At the time we knew her, Iphigenia lived five or six hours from her parents. She was estranged from her only sibling and his family. Iphy and her husband were childless by choice. The center of her life was her marriage, so when she and her husband separated, she was devastated. Then, she got a divorce, a horribly stressful time in anyone's life.

We held her hand through her rage, desolation, feelings of failure and betrayal. She told us her husband had cheated on her with a girlfriend Iphy referred to as Slam Piece. We rallied around her, checking in often, spending as much time with her as we could.

She and her husband had been together since college, so they had become adults together. Most of their friends were either from college or her husband's workplace. We three writing friends seemed to be her only friends *not* connected to her husband. Though she referenced other friends, we never met them, and she referred to us as her "very best friends." In fact, she said we were the reason she decided to remain in the state instead of going back to her beloved hometown. It came as a shock that she'd base her future on staying near us...and to be honest, it made us a little uncomfortable. We told her she should do whatever she wanted, take advantage of her freedom, make some of her dreams come true, go to the place she loved most. No, she said. She wanted to be near us. She loved us, our children and had so many other friends in the area. But these friends were curiously absent; Iphigenia only seemed to have us.

Iphigenia asked us to host a divorce party for her. She was pitching this as her celebration of *finally* getting away from her wretched husband (a change from framing him as the love of her life). "Time to party!" she crowed. We weren't fooled—divorce sucks under the best of conditions, and what with the infidelity, the many times she'd sobbed with grief….but we understood. We went along with her bravado, glad she was trying to start fresh.

So plan a divorce party we did. She told us to expect forty or fifty people—all her friends from work, from college, from life in the town where she'd lived with her husband. We cooked, ordered food, bought wine and spirits to make cocktails. Iphy said her other friends loved a wild shindig. Okay, then. We were there for her.

Six people came to the party. Six. The three of us from the writing group, one of our friends who'd just met Iphy, and a college friend and her brother. It was *heartbreaking*. The college friend made it clear to all of us that she was still friends with Iphy's husband and that there were two sides to every story. She cringed visibly when she saw the "divorce cake," topped with Iphy's special touch—a bride with a beheaded groom, red food coloring pooling on the frosting. The college friend and her brother stayed for less than an hour.

Iphy kept reassuring us that the other friends would come. They didn't. The waiting was agonizing, so we ate and tried to chat and seem like we were having fun. We three were so distressed about these lesser friends who failed to show up for her and so embarrassed for Iphy. She so clearly expected a crowd and a big raucous party. Instead, we sat around the kitchen table, looking at the piles of food, two coolers of wine and drinks, and the enormous cake. It was so, so sad—and enraging.

Where was her family? Where were these other friends? How did forty or fifty people ignore Iphy's invitation? It can't have been that they were all shitty people. Were they ever really her friends? Or had they seen the red flags and, unlike us, steered clear? Mortified for her, we didn't ask, another time we let something slide that should've been addressed.

Red Flag #4: She doesn't respect boundaries.

After the divorce, Iphy moved into a new house and was alone for the first time in her life. She was understandably lonely and really leaned on us. She was available to socialize every weekend, every weeknight, but we all had other obligations—family, kids, jobs, other friends, activities, second jobs.

Not Iphy. She was always free. She texted us often, and during work hours, even when we each asked her not to. Iphy didn't care. Our phones would bleat with her random thoughts, links and images she wanted to share.

Iphy told us she loved being helpful—housesitting especially—but she went so far above and beyond that it became increasingly uncomfortable for us. Once, she dropped by Kristan's place when Kristan and her husband were away. Iphy proceeded to make pancakes for Kristan's teenaged kids, who were being chaperoned by their grandmother. Still, Iphigenia stayed with them for the entire day and stayed for dinner, too. No one knew how to get rid of her, the kids later reported. She stayed and stayed and talked and talked and even vacuumed their grandmother's pool.

When Kristan returned, Iphy told Kristan how much she loved her kids. She then offered to make them the beneficiaries of her life insurance policy. Kristan refused as politely as possible—it was just too much. Iphigenia had a niece and nephew, a brother, parents, other friends and family. Maybe it was simply an impulsive and generous offer, but it had the tingle of bribery to it. Kristan's discomfort grew.

Because Iphy was alone and newly divorced, Kristan invited her to her large annual holiday party. Although Kristan had no intention of matchmaking, a couple of single men were invited. Joss, also single, was there, too. As Iphy left the party, she told Kristan how cute one of her relatives was. Before she was down the driveway, Iphy texted Joss to see if Joss was "okay" with her asking the man out—as if Joss and she were in a contest.

Without waiting for an answer, Iphigenia immediately texted Kristan, asking for the man's number. The relative said he did not want Kristan to give it her, but Iphy was not deterred. "I just want someone to go camping with!" she said. She later asked Kristan to try again, in case the guy ever wanted a "safe camping partner." Kristan told her frankly that he wasn't interested, but Iphy was insistent. Once again, the guy declined to give her his number—awkward all around.

Iphy would often breach Joss's personal space, swinging her feet into Joss's lap, asking Joss to rub them. Joss, who comes across more like the Dowager Countess from *Downton Abbey* than a masseuse, declined. Iphy, who is white, loved Joss's hair. Joss, who is African American, did not want to have her hair touched. Iphy touched anyway.

Red Flag #5: She uses favors as currency.

One afternoon, Iphy stopped at Joss's house unannounced and banged on the door relentlessly. Joss was in the shower at the time, but she heard the commotion and raced downstairs, worried that there was an emergency. "I have to pee," Iphy announced as she charged into Joss's bathroom. She hadn't called or texted beforehand. She just showed up with a full bladder. When Joss said she'd been scared by the banging and asked why couldn't Iphigenia pee at work, Iphy said, "I helped you move in here."

And that was true. She had helped (as had Kristan and Sharon). But Iphy viewed that help as a free pass and brought it up often, reminding Joss that she "owed" Iphy a certain amount of time and intimacy. It was creepy.

Red Flag #6: She lies.

Lying is hard on a friendship. When you first meet people, you don't expect them to lie to you. Why would they, especially when you're becoming friends? But as time went on, Iphy's tales began to show inconsistencies. If questioned —"But you told me X last year and now you're saying Y ... I'm confused," she'd double down. Her "explanations" were exhausting, long and difficult to follow. Iphy would say something along the lines of, "You may have thought I said X, but in fact I said Y, and yet, now that you mention it, X is actually true but so is Y, and have I told you about G yet?"

Putting up with this kind of tap dancing and prevarication was our mistake. Allowing Iphy to feel we had no problem with her contradictions was a lie in itself. We *weren't* okay with it. Our trust was quickly eroding. Everyone exaggerates once in a while, but Iphy was going too far.

She told Kristan she never wanted to be a mom. She told Joss she was unable to have children because of cancer treatments. She told Sharon she was unable to have children because of a *different* medical condition. When Sharon, who holds a PhD in a medical field, contradicted her with an actual fact—Iphy's "condition" was not a medical cause for infertility—Iphy ducked and dodged. The variations in her stories made us uncomfortable. *Can't have children* is very different from *don't want to have children*. Which was true? Why the different explanations? It depended on her mood. One day she'd paint herself as a loner—misunderstood, tragic, betrayed; the next day, it was super fun, cheery, zany, brilliant.

As time passed, the story of her marriage started to crack. One night, she mentioned Gary (not his real name), her husband's best friend. She said she and Gary had fooled around more than once while Iphy was still married.. She was emphatic that it wasn't *technically* cheating—even if most people would *definitely* call it just that. But Iphy believed *her* cheating was forgivable, but her husband finding another woman to love, the so-called Slam Piece, post-divorce as it turns out, was not.

Iphy's marriage was her own business, but she had told us she was the victim of infidelity, when all the while, she'd been cheating with her husband's best friend for *years*. It became increasingly hard for us to be supportive. She'd *lied* to us. When asked about the discrepancies, she would launch into another long, complicated story to justify her actions. By the time we saw this red flag, we'd been friends for years. Had we known the truth from the beginning, that fact alone would've marked her as someone to avoid.

More discrepancies. More tap-dance retellings. More lies.

Iphy once told us about her deep love for her mother-in-law, whom she had nursed through cancer until the bitter end. But then, several years into our friendship, Iphy said she hadn't been permitted to see her mother-in-law during the last few months of her life. She said that when she heard her mother-in-law had died, she bolted from the house barefoot —in the winter—and ran five miles until her feet were bloody. She wasn't allowed at the funeral. This story sounded drastic and hugely different from the tale of the devoted daughter-in-law.

Families can be complicated, but not being "allowed" at a funeral? Why? Huge red flag. Running for five miles in the winter, barefoot, until your feet are *bleeding*? Who *does* that? Huge red flag! Was it truly such a shock to Iphy, a medical professional, that this terminally ill woman had died? Was Iphy a devoted caregiver? Or was she banned from the house? We asked. She dodged, claiming both were true. Sort of. In a way.

It grew increasingly clear that Iphy had a problem with telling the truth. By now, we knew that Iphy was a little off in terms of self-awareness and self-esteem. All of her stories painted her as either hero or victim. Either she was amazing and strong or abused and mistreated because everyone hated her and they were horrible people. Red flag, red flag, red flag.

As hero, Iphy was confident about everything and presented herself as a fun, intelligent person. Her many mysterious, unnamed and unseen friends loved her, she said, yet we never met any of them. Never saw them. Never even heard about her interactions with them. All she told us was that they adored her—yet there was that heartbreaking divorce party of no-shows.

This friendship lasted more than five years. In the beginning, when we saw her sporadically, everything was fine. The flags were barely noticeable. She was a writing critique partner, a friendly acquaintance. As we grew closer, and as her life began to disintegrate, it was difficult to be blunt with her. She'd been through so much. We decided we'd wait for an easier time to discuss the red flags.

That was the wrong call.

We should've talked to her frankly. Each of us—Kristan, Joss and Sharon—had concerns, we found out later, but we didn't share them with each other at the time. Iphigenia was our *friend* (even though it was harder and harder to remember why). We didn't want to gossip even among ourselves. We didn't want to be mean. We didn't want to seem judgmental—which is ridiculous, because of *course* we were judging her! We drew conclusions about her character based on her actions and her accounts of her actions, which is what sentient humans do.

So we just stopped trying to figure her out. We pretended to believe her, her spin, her lies, her stories of Iphigenia, Hero of Everything. We didn't talk with her about her underlying unhappiness or instability. If she said something that struck us as off or was inconsistent with something else she'd told us earlier, we just let it go. It was an unspoken, uncomfortable agreement—let her say what she wants, because getting the truth was too much effort.

You can't keep that shit up. It's exhausting. Your respect and affection erodes. Iphy's manic energy, her outrageous stories and dubious claims were numbing, and expending the effort to call her on it ...well, we were cowards, plain and simple.

So, one by one, we gradually distanced ourselves from her, each doing some lying of her own, independently and unaware the others were doing the same. One of us would say she didn't feel well, another was busy with other things. None of us wanted to cut her off from her only friends, but the truth was, we didn't like her anymore. Our own lives were stable, we had other friendships, families and jobs we loved. We'd just see her through this phase of life, we thought when we finally opened up to each other about Iphy's problems, then hopefully, she'd make more friends and we could gradually fade out.

Should we have talked to each other about the situation sooner? Probably. Sharing concern over a person's mental health is not gossip. It's caring. It took us too long to realize that. We didn't want to be mean girls—in other words, be honest with her—but by trying to avoid that, that's what we became. Mean girls.

Red Flag #7: Her values are different from yours.

When you and your friend disagree on a fundamental level about what defines decency, respect, self-care and kindness, it's impossible to create a deep and lasting bond.

By now, Iphy had revealed herself to be someone who cheated on the husband with his best friend; lied about serious medical issues; self-aggrandized constantly; contradicted her own stories; made impulsive decisions that often involved risks to herself; and didn't respect personal boundaries.

Iphy had a *lot* of stories about men…essentially, how she was always in some flimsy, rom-com situation. She was the occasional caregiver for a disabled girl and had many stories about the parents: the cold, disinterested wife, the compassionate, handsome husband. One time, she told us, she "accidentally" grabbed onto the husband's leg while she sitting on the floor, thinking it was a piece of furniture to steady herself. Ha ha, it was his *leg*! Her mistake! Another time, she had to stay overnight unexpectedly, and she asked him for a t-shirt of his to sleep in. How shocked she was the next morning when he saw her in that thin white t-shirt and nothing else! She acted out how she once had to straddle him to put the child on his lap, and when she bent over, he could see right down her shirt. So uncomfortable, ha ha!

Then there were the times (yes, plural) her bathing suit top came off in the pool, and she didn't even know it! Everyone saw her boobs! And oh, gosh, when the guy cutting the lawn came up on the porch, she was dressed only in a bikini! What timing, right?

We were not *that* stupid. These incidents were no accidents. We questioned her: "Come on, Iphy, how does a person mistake a *human leg* for furniture? And why did you have to sleep in his t-shirt? Why not borrow pajamas from the mom?"

But Iphy dug in, saying, nope, she honestly thought his leg was a chair, and she really and truly didn't know she was flashing the entire gathering at the pool. Et cetera. She relished talking about these incidents, retelling them time and again, always insisting on her complete innocence in every situation. She was never embarrassed or sheepish. Instead, she was proud, oblivious to our discomfort and disbelief.

But …whatcha gonna do? Tell her she sounds fake and irritating? That would be so *mean*. The woman we had first become friends with was a distant memory—the stable, ambitious woman who wanted to be a writer bore little resemblance to the attention-seeking exaggerator we were now dealing with.

Did we eventually suggest counseling? Absolutely. Not for her, she said, and she was adamant.

Red Flag #8: Her emotional reactions are extreme and melodramatic.

Once, when Iphy was angry at her husband, she threw a brick through their glass door. When she found letters that she and her husband had exchanged before they married, she became so hysterical and distraught that Joss nearly called 911.

In her post-divorce life, Iphigenia was on fire to meet the next love of her life. Once again, she asked for her friends' advice—was it too soon to start dating? "Yes," we said. "You need time to adjust, decide what you want in your life, maybe take some classes and think about the next year or two. Take a breath. It's been a helluva year."

Once again, she ignored us. Iphy soon hooked up with a man who owned an inn. Dick (not his real name but absolutely his real personality) made it clear he was not interested in a relationship, but he *would* sleep with her (sometimes). He was up front about the fact that he slept with many women, some of whom were married. (Points for honesty canceled out due to being an asshole.) In addition to his multiple partners, he had two ex-wives and four DUI arrests.

Still, Iphigenia pursued him *ferociously*. We knew running an inn was one of Iphy's pipe dreams, and she couldn't seem to separate her fantasy from the reality of this extraordinarily disgusting man.

She booked one weekend at his inn, then another, then another. No, not to see *Dick*, she'd tell us. To…kayak. Or… because she loved the area, which was a half hour from her house.

Everyone saw through her. Even the manager at the inn told Iphy that Dick was not going to date her and she should back off. But, Iphy explained to us, that manager was another horrible person who clearly hated her.

Or, we thought, the manager was trying to do her a favor.

Iphy just didn't care. Dick was a man. She was sleeping with him. He owned an inn. That seemed to be enough for her. She kept pursuing him. When the governor shut down entire state due to a massive snowstorm, Iphy literally *risked her life* to drive to the inn for the weekend.

After a month or so, Dick had had enough of her. He told her to lose his number. Iphy told us she cried for five straight hours. She wrote him a long, long letter by hand, begging him to reconsider. He refused to see her, but she showed up at his inn nonetheless—with cookies she'd baked.

When Dick lost his license, again, he called her and asked if she'd be his driver. She said yes.

"*Why* do you want to be with him? He's scum!" we told Iphy one memorable evening. "He has four DUIs, he's told you he doesn't want a relationship, he's sleeping with other women! You're going to get an STD, Iphy!"

"Oh, don't worry," she said confidently. "I check him for herpes before we sleep together."

We stared at her, aghast.

That was the breaking point. Her cavalier approach to her health, her relentless defense of her *horrid* non-relationship with Dick along with all of the other red flags we'd shoved under the rug these past five years...it was too much.

The three of us finally did what we should have done before but that had felt so wrong—we talked to each other. We felt horrible—comparing notes, sharing our worries about Iphy's mental health—and, yet, we were so *relieved* that elephant in the room had finally been acknowledged. The old Iphy had seemed so different from the train wreck in front of us, and we each felt guilty about our diminishing affection.

We discussed the best way to approach her. In the end, we chose email, because talking to her was difficult, given her tendency to give long, confusing, contradictory explanations. We also didn't want to invite her out for a social evening and then ambush her with a serious discussion. With an email, we could be succinct and clear. Maybe seeing the truth in black and white would be helpful to her. We signed the email from all three of us, telling her, as kindly and gently as we could, that we were very concerned about her. We then suggested that the next week we could get together and talk about things face to face.

Let us be clear. It is nothing short of *agonizing* to write such a letter. We told her up front that the email would be very hard to read but that we loved her and wanted the best for her. But, we wrote, we could no longer pretend that her actions were okay. We hoped that because we were her closest friends, by her own admission, that she'd think carefully about what we were saying.

The letter contained our concerns about her manic activities, the goals she had dropped, the horrible interactions with Dick, the contradictions in so many pivotal stories. We suggested counseling and seeing a physician to see if medication might be in order.

Iphy responded within the hour. She was receptive to our concerns, she said, and we were indeed her closest friends and she wanted to listen. She was grateful that we cared so much, but it would be helpful if we sent specific examples.

We had talked about it—should we go into detail? We didn't think we should, given her history of defending her choices with every breath. We wrote back saying that if she was truly happy and her life was on track, we were happy for her but we needed to step back, because there were fundamental differences between us.

She insisted. She really, really wanted to know what red flags we were talking about. She claimed to have no idea what we we were talking about. With trepidation, we sent a few examples, repeating that if she felt these were good life choices, that was fine, but we couldn't pretend that we agreed.

Iphy had shown us in the past how she reacted to any perceived disapproval—by doubling down. This time was no different. Within a couple of hours, she sent us several very, very long responses. She lashed out, insisting her life was exactly how she wanted it. The relationship with the innkeeper was "unconventional" and "nontraditional." She *loved* her job and viewed her work as nearly sacred ...never mind what she'd said before, never mind her desire to return to teaching or her dream of writing a book.

She told us that she showed the email to her other friends —those people we had never met, who failed to show up for her divorce party, whose names she never mentioned—and they were *stunned* by our cruelty. Once again, Iphy was the innocent victim of very horrible people. This time, those horrible people were us three. She never wanted to see us again.

And that, readers, was a tremendous relief. It was hard, knowing we had severed a friendship, but, really, what kind of friendship was it? A *really* crappy one. Did we miss her? The honest truth is no. Did we feel guilty about that? Of course. No one wants to be in the position of saying, "At the end of the day, I just don't like or respect you." But it was the truth.

Our Mistakes

Talking with each other about our time with Iphy, we realized there was a lot we could've done better. Through her actions, she had shown us, repeatedly, who she was, and we didn't want to see it.

Protecting our own egos may well have been part of the reason it took so long for us to draw the line in the sand. We *wanted* to be the magical friends who could fix her issues, make her feel loved, make her slow down, focus, be successful and happy. Of course, we lacked that power. No one can change another person. You cannot fix a person and make her whole with your love and friendship, advice and guidance. Only she has that power.

Another reason for our flawed response had to do with timing. Right about the time the red flags were really flying, Iphy told us about her divorce. We couldn't back off then.

What kind of person leaves when her friend's life is in the shitter? Not us! We were better than that! We could stick it out. And we did, and maybe it was the right call, but it did foster Iphy's unrealistic belief that we were all very close friends.

Another part was our own laziness. We could endure an occasional evening with Iphy (until we couldn't). It was easier than confronting our discomfort, disbelief, disappointment. A few hours of our lives ...so what? Speaking up would be too hard, so we put it off as long as we could. Not consciously, perhaps. We hadn't planned on ending our friendship. She did that. But we had finally drawn the line in the sand. *If you think these behaviors are okay, please accept that we do not, and we can't pretend otherwise any longer.*

In our efforts to be good friends, we committed a sin of friendship—we were untruthful about our feelings. We had a crappy friend, and we *were* crappy friends. It felt horrible to realize this, but realizing it was healthy, too. It was a way to learn from our mistakes, to avoid ever getting enmeshed with someone who was draped in red flags, to be more honest going forward and to steer clear of anyone whose priorities and values don't match up with ours.

Our experience with Iphy had a huge impact on us all. We became slightly obsessed with the myriad, layered issues in female friendships. The experience allowed us to see that we can and *should* set boundaries and expect them to be respected. Friendship doesn't give someone permission to run roughshod over you. You don't have to be friends with people just because they express an interest in you. You are not obliged to spend time with *anyone* who makes you feel uncomfortable.

Iphy, we hope you're living your best life, surrounded by people who love and value you. We're sorry we weren't honest with you sooner. Take good care of yourself.

DRAPED IN RED FLAGS: LESSONS FROM THE TRENCHES

1. She doesn't have other female friends.
2. She asks for help and advice and then refuses to take it.
3. No one else shows up for her.
4. She doesn't respect boundaries.
5. She uses favors as currency.
6. She lies.
7. Her values are different from yours.
8. Her emotional reactions are extreme and melo-dramatic.

CHAPTER 5

BITCHERY

SINCE WE LADIES STARTED THE CRAPPY FRIENDS podcast in 2018, we've gotten many letters that circle the theme of generalized bitchery. We all know the term "toxic friend," but what does it mean, really? For us, it means a friend who drains you of positivity. There's no reciprocity of love, interest and kindness. Your so-called friend makes you feel *worse* about things, rather than better, and she does so deliberately.

That's the key. It's deliberate. She's no friend.

You ain't got time for bitchery, honey. Heed our words.

So, in this chapter, let's focus on the kind of bitchery that manifests as envy, jealousy and cruelty. This type of deliberate bitchery has a tendency to sneak up on you and take a shot at your heart before you know what's what. And while it may feel like the behavior came out of nowhere, we Ladies have found that envy, jealousy, and the resulting passive-aggression usually have been there from the beginning, undiagnosed and growing like a weed. If you can relate to the experiences in the following, then great., gold star for you! Bonus points if you recognize yourself as the perpetrator of harmful bitchery. Feeling wronged is one thing. Admitting that you've wronged is quite another.

Envy

We received a letter from one of our listeners, Dirty Sock, who had lately been going through a really rough time and resented her friends for their seemingly trouble-free lives. Trouble oftentimes comes in threes, and boy, did it ever for Dirty Sock. She had a miscarriage, and two months later, her mom died in a car accident. In the middle of all of that, the frequency of fights between Dirty Sock and her boyfriend of seven years had increased. He was uncomfortable with her grief, and so they broke up. If that wasn't enough, Dirty Sock moved to a new town and accepted a lateral transfer to a position that didn't challenge her at all.

Wow. Just wow.

Where were her friends in all this, you ask? They showed up at first, Dirty Sock explained in her letter, but now she felt like they had a bit of compassion fatigue. Seeing how fabulous their lives seemed didn't help her at all. One had just had a baby, another finished her master's degree and got a promotion, and yet another met a great guy online and married him.

Teddy Roosevelt once said, "Comparison is the thief of joy." Man had a point, but Dirty Sock was still missing her mother, still waking up at night from dreams that she was still engaged to her seven-year boyfriend. It's hard not to envy the luck others have when all of yours seems like it's run out.

Dirty Sock's coping mechanism was to hate on her friends. The friend who just got married? DS thought about seducing her husband. He was hot, so what the hell. The friend with the new baby? DS wanted to tell her how ugly the baby was. And she wanted to call her diverse group of friends racists. She wanted to smack the smugness right off their faces because she wanted a baby, a fab husband and a great job too.

She wanted what her friends had and resented them for having it— the very definition of envy.

In Dirty Sock's case, her envy was fairly benign—she never took any of those actions she thought about. Her feelings were seeded by all of her completely understandable troubles. Untreated, this situation could've easily escalated into estrangement and friendship chasms too wide to bridge.

How to Deal with Your Feelings of Envy

1. Suss out the root cause.
For Dirty Sock, the root cause of her envy was the tragedy and grief that sat on her shoulders like a boulder. She recognized that these feelings paralyzed her, kept her from any positive forward motion and easily let negativity through.

2. Take action.
Ask yourself what you can do, right now, to alleviate some of the symptoms. Maybe you envy your buddy's professional success. Can you shine up your resume and find a new job? Can you take a class that would help you meet your own professional goals? Maybe you envy your friend's fulfilling relationship. Consider volunteering or joining a group that helps you to meet like-minded people—a book club or a dating site or a nonprofit organization that needs help getting the word out. Get out of your own head. Envy can consume you if you let it, so don't.

3. Enlist your friends' help.
Chances are your friends know when something's up with

you. Dirty Sock's friends did and they were looking for an opportunity to step up. Their "compassion fatigue" was Dirty Sock's interpretation of matters—an incorrect one, which isn't surprising. Grief can be tricky, layering insecurity and anger on top of sadness until you can't see what's real. Good friends *want* to be there for each other. They may not know *how* in the moment, but the spirit is definitely willing. After Dirty Sock told her friends the truth about how she was feeling, that she still really needed them, they came through with flying colors, promising to text daily to make sure she was doing okay, and if she wasn't, scheduling some healing girl time. The lesson here is to be specific about your needs. Envy your friend's great job? Ask her if she can help you network. We Ladies are betting she'll jump at the chance to drum up a lead or three for you. Wish you had a guy like your friend's? The Ladies would bet cash-money that your friend will be your wingman, rewrite your dating profile or interview their own boyfriend's friends to help you find Mr. or Ms. Right (or Right Now).

Jealousy

We all love drama. When you found out that *Game of Thrones* villain Cersei Lannister was sleeping with her twin brother and that all three of her children were fathered by him, you screamed at the TV and then took to social media to find out WTabsoluteF. Okay, maybe that was just us, but you get the idea.

Drama can be thrilling. It's fun to speculate about what that shady woman at work is actually up to, but when drama is a regular part of your life, interfering with your vacation plans, family events or just your day-to-day life, it becomes a real problem. During those times it can be impossible to see that drama is ruling your life. You spend so much time reacting to each situation that you can't see the big picture.

That's exactly what was happening with our listener Fed Up in Ohio who started her letter to us with, "I have a sister who is two years younger than me and suffice it to say I pretty much hate her." Okay then.

Competition between Fed Up and her sister Sharla (not her real name) existed since they were babies, nurtured by their mother's favoritism. Sharla is the golden child, a fact her mother repeats to Fed Up during their daily phone calls. Sharla is a lawyer and works on many important pro bono cases. She adopted a child from foster care. To their mother, Sharla is a goddess, while Fed Up is "only" a happily married stay-at-home mom.

Maybe Fed Up could've ignored the deification of Sharla if her younger sister had been a fun, loving confidante, but she wasn't. She was sanctimonious and judgmental and found passive-aggressive ways to remind Fed Up that she wasn't good enough. "Oh, you send your children to private school? I think it's important that my child have a real-world experience." "Oh, you're still not working? How *do* you fill your day?"

Mom's favoritism, fed by Sharla's sense of superiority, created real jealousy. The Merriam-Webster dictionary defines jealousy as "hostility toward a rival or one believed to enjoy an advantage." Both Sharla and Fed Up feared losing out to the other. If Sharla had a success, Fed Up hurried to detail her own success, even though she resented having to do it. For Fed Up, hearing about Sharla's fabulousness was like hearing nails on a chalkboard. The Ladies suspect that it was the same for Sharla. Otherwise why would she continue to bait Fed Up every time the sisters spoke?

Buddhism teaches that negative mental states are comprised of three poisons: ignorance, hate and greed. The one most in play between Fed Up and her sister is ignorance. Their ignorance is clear from their perceptions of each other

—Fed Up thinks that Sharla's life is perfect, Sharla thinks that Fed Up's life is hollow. These are, at the very least, incomplete views of each other's reality.

The thing about ignorance is that it's static. Willfully remaining ignorant of the facts of a situation sets your feet in concrete and allows for no learning, no forward motion. All you have at your disposal is your own analysis, which is hardly the full picture.

Say your loved one forgets your birthday or anniversary. Do you fume, thinking this person is thoughtless and unkind? As the hours progress without recognition, do your thoughts escalate until, in your mind, your loved one is the most inconsiderate person you know? After all, there is proof! No card! No gift! And there you are, stuck in your loop of ignorance and self-pity...when the card or gift shows up later.

Maybe something pretty damn significant had caused your person to forget your day. Maybe she was going through some serious shit of her own. You will likely feel small hearted about your resentment if you learn that someone close to her had just died, or she'd been fired. You don't know what you don't know. Try not to make assumptions.

How to Deal with Feelings of Jealousy

1. Become more self-aware.
Knowing who you are and how others see you can go a long way to alleviating jealous feelings. Make a list of your positive qualities. Are you kind? Do you live your life with integrity? Do your friends and family view you as a good person— funny, reliable, brave, decent? Insecurity and fear will have a hard time taking root in your psyche if you know that you are worthy of love and respect.

2. Show "comparison" the exit.

Teddy Roosevelt's wise words bear repeating: "Comparison is the thief of joy." Sure, your friend is successful and seems to have it all, but *her life is not the only definition of success.* Beware of critical thoughts and define success on your own terms. Think about the ways you have been able to not just survive, but thrive. Have you DIY-ed the hell out of your small apartment? Your creative and nimble mind is your triumph. Why be jealous of your friend's McMansion when your cozy living room, which could be an Instagram sensation, makes you feel happy and loved? Strive for your personal best and then cheer your friend on as she strives for hers.

3. Challenge the hell out of your assumptions.

Fed Up has heard endlessly about her sister's amazing life. Is it amazing, though? Fed Up had not been getting her information from a reliable source. She assumed that her mother's version of events was the truth, which is an easy mistake to make. Fed Up got along with her mother swimmingly when Sharla was not in the picture, so why wouldn't she assume that her mother's word was gospel? Don't get us wrong—we Ladies don't believe that Fed Up's mother was being malicious or was even conscious of the discord her favoritism sowed between her daughters. Maybe Mom just thought she was relaying information, like any proud mama would. She probably didn't hear the unspoken criticism Fed Up was hearing as she sang Sharla's praises. When Mom said, "Sharla does so much rewarding pro bono work," Fed Up heard *Why can't you be more like her?*

Fight your assumptions with a healthy dose of compassion and honesty. In fact, be as compassionate as you can until you have solid information to contradict it. Thinking that her sister was holier-than-thou and judgmental lead Fed

Up to follow this line of thinking: *Why does my sister say judgey things to me? It's because she thinks she's better than me!* A compassionate view would have led her to a different conclusion: *Maybe she thinks I'm the one with the superiority complex, so she says passive-aggressive things to take me down a notch. Wait, that's actually what I do to her! Oh. Huh.*

Using this technique to see events and interactions through new eyes can be relieving and oddly satisfying. It is also a good first step toward healing—if not your relationship, then yourself.

4. Do Not Act Out

For the love of all that's holy, DO NOT ACT ON YOUR JEALOUS FEELINGS. Jealous thoughts are normal to some extent. Jealous actions? Hoo boy! Stop! Full stop! If you feel yourself getting riled up, we Ladies implore you not to go out in the middle of the night and slash your friend's tires. Instead, talk to someone you trust to remind yourself of your successes and your worth and, most important, to see how baseless your assumptions are. Maybe that trusted person is a therapist. Maybe it's a mutual friend. Maybe it's even the very person you're jealous of.

In a perfect world, your BFF knows that sometimes you suffer from insecurity. She understands that sometimes you just need a little propping up to get you past whatever triggered your jealousy. Because sometimes, she's a little jealous of you too.

Take us Ladies, for example. Kristan is married, has two children and makes her living as a writer. Joss is single, childless by choice and balances writing with a day job. Certainly, there are times when Kristan fantasizes about having the freedom of a single person, the reassuring structure of a regular job, the money she would've saved if she didn't have kids. And certainly, there are times when Joss wishes she had a partner who could fix shit, two lovely children who shared her interests, and the freedom to make her own writing schedule.

We're both right. We both have happy lives. Yet we both wonder about the road not taken. And we can talk about it. The feelings of jealousy do not have to fester and become something destructive.

We Ladies advised Fed Up to have a conversation with her sister, without Mom in the middle, a conversation that prioritized compassion and honesty and allowed a little bit of vulnerability. A sister's weekend, we suggested, might reveal all and lead to the beginning of a beautiful friendship.

Cruelty

Friendships that span decades are special for so many reasons. This friend you've known for most of your life has seen you through many ups and downs. She knows all your secrets because she was there with vodka and chocolate when some stupid man broke your heart. She probably suspected you were pregnant before you did. When she was weak after surgery, you cooked meals, washed her hair and took her kids to school. If for any reason, you lost the ability to speak, you are pretty sure your friend could speak for you with reliable accuracy.

This was the kind of friendship our listener Betrayed wrote that she had with Matilda (not her real name) that is, until Matilda stabbed Betrayed in the back.

Betrayed's marriage was slowly disintegrating. The reason wasn't earth-shattering or scandalous, just two people gradually growing apart. Betrayed also wrote that Matilda's husband was wonderful, had always been wonderful. In fact, Betrayed had once mentioned to Matilda, fifteen or so years back, that her husband was the *best*. Even now, their friend group—women in their neighborhood—agreed that Matilda had picked a winner.

Naturally, Betrayed confided in Matilda while her marriage was breaking apart. Again, there was no real animosity between Betrayed and her husband. According to Betrayed, "My husband and I figure we can get along better if I'm not hating on him because he takes baths and doesn't rinse his pubic hair out of the tub, and he doesn't have to bitch about my cooking and my father who never liked him."

Finally, Betrayed told Matilda that she and her husband decided to divorce. Instead of showing the compassion and kinship that had been part of their friendship for twenty-five years, Matilda *blamed* Betrayed for the breakup. The demise of the marriage was all Betrayed's fault, Matilda said. She claimed Betrayed just didn't know how to treat a good man. She ended her tirade by saying, "No wonder he cheated on you!"

Wait. What?

Yep, apparently Betrayed's husband had been cheating on her for *years*. Matilda had known and had said nothing about it. (We were like, *Are you freakin' serious right now?)*

Following that, Matilda told their friend group that Betrayed was in love with Matilda's husband. She froze Betrayed out of the group, making sure she got to all the friends in the group before Betrayed could explain her side of the story. Newly divorced, Betrayed now found herself ostracized in the neighborhood where she'd lived for decades, by the very friends she loved most.

Betrayed's mother called Matilda a "turd." (We couldn't agree more.) But that didn't help Betrayed, who felt confused, brokenhearted and, despite everything, really missed her friend. For Betrayed, the death of her friendship was much worse than the end of her marriage.

This kind of cruelty doesn't come out of nowhere. Decades of friendship—all the good and hard times—make it difficult to see where the cracks are in the relationship, but they're definitely there. Mean girls like Matilda are easy to recognize because of the corpses of dead friendships and estrangements in their past. We Ladies were certain that Matilda didn't suddenly become mean. She had always been that way. Betrayed had checked certain boxes in Matilda's world. Once Betrayed was no longer married, Matilda had no use for her.

When you're deep in a friendship with someone like that, you don't think twice about their eye-rolling or mean remarks because you're so focused on the friendship. Maybe you hear their snarky comments about someone as attempts to be funny, not vicious, and excused them. *She's tired, she's having a bad day,* or *she's usually so nice/generous/giving that this must be a one-off.*

No, honey. It's not a one-off. It's the kind of red flag that should warn you to keep your distance or, at the very least, only socialize with this person casually and give up on the idea of a real friendship . (See the list of red flags in Chapter 4.)

Contempt for and devaluation of others are signs that your friend is missing key attributes of compassion and empathy. If you yourself think and act with compassion and empathy, you'll notice when others don't. Spotting this red flag early will help you avoid wasting time on someone without those positive traits.

How to Combat the Cruelty of "Friends"

1. Heed the warning signs.

Having been there ourselves, we Ladies advise that you

listen to your instincts from the start. Pay attention to all red flags as they appear on the friendship highway. Trust your gut. If your friend behaves in a way that makes you squint with confusion or cock your head, pay attention. If she often leads with a qualifier (*I'm not usually so mean, but* ...or *You know I hate to gossip, but* ...or *OMG, was that catty? I can't believe I said that!*). PAY ATTENTION. She is showing you who she is.

Systemic bitchery, we Ladies have found, always has a source. No baby is born mean and spiteful. Hurt people hurt people, as the saying goes. It's not your job to fix them. You're not a bad person for stepping away. But you may feel like you need more evidence before you condemn a burgeoning friendship to the trash heap—and that's fine— but don't ignore early warning signs.

If your friend's bad behavior is a one-time event, however, try to view it compassionately instead of speculating about her motives. (When we Ladies say "one time," we mean one time. If her bitchy behavior is a habitual thing, you need to skip to steps 2 and 3 below.)

When you view your friend's behavior with compassion, you are encouraging trust and intimacy within your friendship. Think about it. Your friend lashes out at you, and instead of shouting "You bitch!" you say, "I know you're having a tough time at work/with your mother/with your boyfriend, do you wanna talk/get together/eat chocolate." If your friend can acknowledge her behavior and lean into your compassionate attitude, it's a positive sign. Your compassion and empathy may help you both reframe a potentially off-balance situation, which, in turn, may ultimately promote stability in your friendship.

But if your friend's bitchy behavior becomes habitual, if your friend considers your compassionate acceptances as her due and doesn't return the favor, we Ladies are seriously side-eyeing her.

2. Speak up.

Let's say you're in the thick of a longtime friendship and you wake up one day and realize, "This woman is actually a crappy person." For years, you've laughed with her while she said cruel things while secretly feeling exhausted by it. For years, you've been part of her club—which means that you've tacitly agreed with her behavior, doesn't it? Now you're in the position of wanting to pull back. You can still set some boundaries to unstick yourself from a friendship that makes you feel like you're trapped in quicksand.

Address objectionable behavior when it happens. Don't like the way your friend speaks about someone? Don't let it go. Don't attribute it to her having a bad day. In that moment, say, "Hey, that's not cool. Please don't say [or do] that again." Your friend's reaction will tell you *everything* you need to know about her character. If she says, "Shit, you're right" and apologizes, that's the appropriate response, and you can go from there.

If, instead, she says, "Oh, lighten up," explain to her that this sort of mean behavior makes you uncomfortable. If she points out that her cruelty has never made you uncomfortable before, tell her it's making you uncomfortable now. If you hold this line *every time,* your relationship will either become fuller and richer or it will fade away.

Mind you, we both have been in friendships where we've tried this approach, when we've felt that speaking up and pointing out bitchy behavior could help stop or change it. Sometimes, it has. Other times, not so much. At those times, the friend might give lip service to regretting her behavior —"Gosh golly, did I say that? So sorry!" But the resentment at being called out builds, the friendship grows toxic, and her meanness is turned on you.

If that happens, move on. Remember, it's not your job to fix her. You couldn't even if you wanted to.

3. Pull the knife out of your back.

Maybe, like Betrayed, you've been completely blindsided by your friend's true nature. How do you recover?

First, acknowledge your grief and let that process unfold without judging yourself. Avoid thoughts like, "She was just a friend, so why am I so broken up about this?" or, "I should be over this by now." The loss of a decades-long friend is a major life event! Your feelings are completely valid—so much so that medical professionals often ask about friendship loss during a mental health screening, as happened with Joss.

Give yourself permission to grieve the friendship's demise. Be kind to yourself. Create a self-care routine that helps you to heal and that includes exercise, massage, nutritious foods, and the spiritual nutrients you might get from meditation or a religious service or walks in nature. Read. Honor those parts of you that feel eternal in whatever way works for you. Don't be shy about asking for more emotional support from your healthy relationships. Perhaps you might consider therapy. And definitely schedule some time to Netflix and chill with Ben and Jerry (or mac and cheese—or both).

Acknowledge that going over and over the situation in your mind is normal and often necessary. You have to get the confused feelings out of your system, to stop kicking yourself over those choice words you came up with three weeks too late, those red flags you should never have ignored. Once you've done that ten or fifty times, that's enough. Remind yourself that in the end, the result is the same. The "friendship" is dead.

When you're ready, get back out there and make some new friends. Use the lessons you've learned from this toxic friendship to inform you as you navigate the paths to healthy relationships. Don't use the bad experience as a reason to hide. Don't retreat or erect boundaries covered with electrified barbed wire and spikes. Your goal as you grieve is not to be broken by your experience, but to metabolize aspects that are valuable and/or informative, and to excrete the waste.

More than anything else, compassion for yourself can help you heal when you've stepped in it big time.

CHAPTER 6

ATTENTION WHORES AND
DRAMA MAMAS

OH, THAT FRIEND OF YOURS! SHE'S AMAZING! AT FIRST,
you roar with laughter at her stories, marvel at her wisdom,
enjoy her shenanigans. She's the life of the party! She *always*
has a great tale to tell. She's larger than life, and in the beginning, you have a blast together.

But after a not very long time, you begin to see that the
spotlight has to be on her, always. You, on the other hand,
don't even know there is a spotlight.

Everyone loves a good storyteller to be sure. But Attention Whores aren't telling stories for your entertainment or
because they want to share their experiences with you, their
close friend. They're telling stories in order to be on center
stage.

Attention Whores

Once upon a time, Kristan took a friend out to a lovely,
quiet restaurant for dinner. Tonya (not her real name) talked
the entire time (about herself, her work, her family, her life,
her pets, her romances). Kristan had known this friend for

years, but when they were together there was none of that comfortable camaraderie or sharing of memories, as you might expect. The friend simply held forth. Absolutely anyone could've been sitting in the chair across from Tonya during that dinner. In fact, a cardboard cutout could've been sitting across from Tonya, and Kristan is not sure Tonya would've noticed (and Kristan could've happily been home, reading, instead).

Tonya is a classic Attention Whore (AW). If the conversation isn't about her, she makes sure it is—and in short order. If someone else was talking, Tonya would bide her time, impatiently, until it was once again her turn to talk. Even if she had told the story before, Tonya would let it rip once again. Sure, you might be going through something tough, or have exciting news, or be wicked sad, but, really, every encounter is all about Tonya.

Tonya, hindsight showed, lacked a fundamental interest in other people. To be honest, she didn't even care that much about Kristan, a fact that became quite clear. During the friendship, though, Kristan made excuses for Tonya: "Yeah, but she's …entertaining?" Tonya didn't have many other friends (Hello? Red flag!), and Kristan felt a bit sorry for her. She knew Tonya was exaggerating because her real life hadn't turned out as planned. (Hint: there are no true friendships based on pity.)

AWs usually have big personalities. They *can* be great storytellers and have oodles of confidence that, yes, they are the most interesting person in the room (they never are.) But they believe they are, and at first, you might think so, too.

AWs hate to fail, because failure goes against what they believe about themselves, down to their bone marrow: *I am the best, smartest, prettiest, funniest, most talented person ever and I deserve everything.* And hey! We Ladies never want to fault a woman for being confident— but we give credit where it's due. We tend to believe compliments about someone when *other people* say them. Your friend saying, "I'm so generous!" has a lot less credibility than someone else whispering to you, "She's so generous" when said friend is in the loo.

When confidence is not backed up by real-life evidence, it may be a symptom of an inflated ego, or narcissism. And narcissists *can* be charming. You might think you'll learn something from this person. You might truly enjoy her company. But as time goes on, you realize there's not a lot a whole lot there—which is the exact opposite of what the AW wants you to think.

The problem with being friends with an AW is that she can never get enough attention, and the "friendship" is oddly impersonal (as in "cardboard cutout," above). She'll tire of you—and she may tire of you quickly, in fact, because you're not really a person to her. You're a member of her audience.

Of course, as with most AWs, there's a deep-seeded insecurity lurking deep beneath the surface. Maybe she really did believe she was the best, only to then have the world tell her, "Um …not so much." Bitterness stews. God forbid you're more successful on the same playing field. Be careful. She will cut you. She's probably unaware of her insecurity—it's the world that's at fault in not recognizing her magnificence, silly. And if the world recognizes you instead, duck. For example, when Kristan won an award for one of her books, her AW friend, also a writer, never spoke to her again. Which was perfectly okay, to be honest.

AWs are incapable of admitting wrongdoing, so lying is often a characteristic of this personality type. How many times has an AW friend claimed she missed your social media post about your promotion, couldn't make it to your birthday party, never spread that rumor about you? A lot of times, that's how many.

Some of our listeners have written in to ask how to fix a friendship with an AW. Unfortunately, even with our crystal ball, we Ladies don't have great news. It's possible (though perhaps not probable) that underneath the AW's endless spotlight hogging, there's a heart of gold—although if you've been in the friendship long enough, you'd likely have seen that. Still, an honest conversation in which you tell your friend you need equal time, a little less of her grandstanding, might send her a blast of self-awareness. Don't bet on it, though.

We have a mutual friend who excels at telling funny stories. Many are the times when we are side-eyed by other patrons in a movie theater or restaurant because we are laughing uncontrollably, courtesy of our storytelling pal. But the *first* thing we noticed about her was her heart of gold. The storytelling was just gravy. She is not a spotlight hog or an Attention Whore. She's compassionate, kind *and* funny— and you can spot all that a mile away.

Drama Mamas

Not all Attention Whores are Drama Mamas, but all Drama Mamas are Attention Whores.

Say again?

Well, all border collies are dogs, but not all dogs are border collies.

The Drama Mama (DM) wants attention, too, but she gets it in a different way. She's not grandstanding or telling the funniest story. Instead, she is emotional. Very emotional. A lot. You may not realize this, however, until you are figuratively (and perhaps literally) pounding on her door for a safety check. She hasn't returned your texts, calls, emails, and you honestly have no idea why

The reason is, she *wants* you banging on her door,

begging her to talk to you. She wants you to know she is in pain and she wants you to try to cure her (which she won't let you do, FYI, because then she would lose her power, which comes from being in pain).

Why is she doing this shit?

She likes the attention, and she doesn't think she can get it any other way. God forbid you just got some positive attention—a promotion, a record deal, a lottery win, your spouse surprising you with flowers, a compliment from a stranger—it could be anything. DMs are in competition with everyone, including you. They just don't want you to know it.

DMs have two styles of modus operandi: the secret hurt and withdrawal that incites you to worry for their mental and physical health (see "door pounding," above) and the explosive rage. "That's it! I'm done!" she might bellow, seemingly from out of nowhere. She flounces out the door, blocks you from her phone, calls all your mutual friends and complains, pleased to have peed on your parade, waiting for you to prostrate yourself for your unknown wrongdoing.

Let's say you and your friend Gillian (not her real name) work at the same large company. You met as coworkers but have since become close friends (or so you think). You talk about work and share what you know. Gillian, on the other hand, does *not* share. And if you ask her for a favor, she'd love to help, but she's so busy. Need insight into something? She'll claim not to have any. But that's just her. Whatever. She's your friend. She can be fun. You don't mind (except you do).

The day comes when you're asked to give a presentation to the big bosses who are flying in from France, and you work night and day on it, making sure it is impeccable and insightful. The big day comes, and you ace it. The big bosses are dazzled, congratulatory, grateful. It's a great day for you.

Your manager takes everyone out for dinner …but where's Gillian? Surely she'd want to come, too. Right?

Wrong. She has a migraine. She doesn't answer your first seven texts, so your big night is tainted with worrying whether she's okay, and that's *exactly* as she wants it. Later, she's cool toward you. You sense the tremor in the Force and decide to ask her.

And then comes the unleashing. Oh, how you have wronged her! She has thirty-nine examples of times you let her down, didn't include her, said something awkward, smiled too much, didn't smile enough.

Guess what? No matter what you say next, you'll never be friends again. You never were, sweetheart. The "friendship" has always only been about when you could help her. All those times when you shared and commiserated were her mining you for information so she could get ahead.

The drama mama cannot let you have your moment. She's the bridesmaid who ruins your bachelorette party by telling you tearfully that she fell in love with your fiancé first. She announces she's had a huge fight with her sister upon entering your hospital room, barely looking at your newborn twins. Or maybe she doesn't show up to see the wee bairns at all, too consumed with her drama to share your happiness. Did your book just hit a bestseller list? DM can't congratulate you, because something awful just happened to her.

One of our listeners wrote to us about a friend, Horrentia (not her real name) who had a tantrum when two strangers didn't take her advice about where to eat. The letter writer and Horrentia were having a perfectly pleasant evening when two tourists asked if they knew of a good restaurant. Horrentia recommended the place where they had just eaten. "I'm a local," she said. "I know where the best food is." The tourists perused the menu, then—for whatever reason— opted to keep walking. Horrentia exploded. "You're stupid if you don't listen to me!" she shouted. "I grew up here! I know the best places!"

Our letter writer was mortified. Why did Horrentia take their decision so personally? There are a number of reasons the tourists might have passed on the place—food allergies, cost, crowds, an ex-husband lurking within, whatever. It was their business! The letter writer wondered why Horrentia reacted that way.

The reason is because she felt disrespected. Horrentia prized being a local. She wanted to be seen as *the* authority on food in the area. When the tourists opted against her recommendation, she felt invalidated—which is ridiculous. She called the people "stupid,"

and her rage and disproportionate reaction marked her as insecure, childish and unpleasant. Our listener admitted it wasn't the first time Horrrentia had acted that way, and we explained that it wouldn't be the last.

Is there any way to reason with a friend like that?

Well, you can always try the "when you do X, I feel Y" approach, which lets your friend know what effect her actions have on you. *When you scream at tourists, I feel mortified. When you lose control, I feel uncertain and nervous about your temper.* It's possible that people like Horrentia aren't aware of their effect on others, but we Ladies think it's probable that Horrentia and her kind are *absolutely* aware of it. Their behavior gives them a sense of power. Horrentia was rejected, at least in her own version of the narrative, so she lashed out at the "stupid" tourists to save face. Why was it so important that her suggestion be taken? Her insecurity.

There is no age limit on insecurity, and it manifests itself in different ways. The Attention Whore grabs the microphone in a death grip because otherwise the spotlight might go to someone else, and she'll be overlooked. The Drama Mama subtly undercuts her friend's achievements because they outshine hers. She cannot stand to be overlooked (even in something as small as a restaurant recommendation).

Listen, sweetheart. That shit gets old. Maya Angelou, our queen, said, "When someone shows you who they are, believe them the first time." That goes for the kind, generous, welcoming people as well as the assholes. Judge people by their actions.

Without counseling, insecurity is damn hard to fix. (We say this as insecure people who've each had counseling.) Insecurity comes from difficult experiences we have had that make us feel unimportant, overlooked or ignored—that made us feel small. Insecurity may stem from childhood experiences, or from the feeling that the world not does not recognize your gifts. Maybe at times you've *been* the insecure friend. We both have also held that role. *Does she really like me, or does she feel sorry for me? Am I a part of this group, or am I bothering people? When she said X, was she talking about me?*

How to Combat Your Own Feelings of Insecurity

1. Think about the person who made you feel insecure and try to discern the reason. What was going on in her life that made you feel small and insignificant, whether she meant to or not?

2. See yourself through the eyes of someone who loves you, whether that's a parent, sibling, partner or friend. There's a beautiful scene in *This Is Us* when teenager Kate resents her dad for secretly filming her while she is singing. She hates seeing herself—she's not skinny enough, she looks like a dork, etc. But later, she realizes her father is seeing the most beautiful, talented, lovely girl in

the world, the person he loves so much. Embrace that person.

3. Affirm yourself. "I'm good enough, smart enough, and gosh darn it! People like me!" as the SNL character Stuart Smalley would say to his reflection in the mirror. Sure, that's a start. But also try this: *My opinion matters just as much as anyone's.* Or *People seek me out for advice because I'm sensible and kind.* Or *I was invited because they like me and enjoy my company.*

4. Be good to yourself. (If we were all kinder to ourselves, there'd be a lot fewer AWs and DMs out there.) Treat yourself as you would treat your best friend. If you're tired, give yourself permission to take a nap. If you're lonely, pick up the phone and call someone you like talking to. Splurge on something that you've wanted for a long time and can finally afford. It's all well and good to chill with Netflix and chocolate ice cream, but that sort of treat can drift into a self-numbing habit pretty quickly. Use those things as a reward, not a coping mechanism. You'll enjoy them more.

CHAPTER 7

FRENEMIES

FRENEMY, NOUN.

Someone who is both friend and enemy; a relationship that is both mutually beneficial or dependent while being competitive, fraught with risk and mistrust.

—Urban Dictionary

Frenemies are those people who seem nice on the surface but have ulterior motives. Someone who praises you one moment, but spreads gossip about you the next. Someone you are never quite sure is on your side. Sometimes she is, but sometimes she's not. You can never shake the nagging feeling that she'll throw you under the bus at a moment's notice.

And you're right. She will.

We've had letters about this type of not-a-friend—the person you asked to be a bridesmaid and then did her utter best to ruin on your wedding. Gillian in the previous chapter, who can't be happy that you're exceling at work because she thinks it takes away from her own performance. The person who befriends you the first day of grad school, then, when your grades are better, starts a whisper campaign about you with your fellow classmates. The woman who freezes you out because that cute chick hit on you at the bar the other night.

A frenemy is usually competing with you on some level —schooling, profession, social status. She gets you, in that she understands your perspective, goals and issues, but she uses that knowledge to manipulate situations to her own benefit. She can seem like a great pal at first, always listening and asking the important questions—but don't be fooled! She's only interested in how you can advance *her*. She may lie. She may poach your ideas. She'll be just nice enough to make you believe she is your friend. Sister, don't be naive.

In high school, she was the girl who was only nice to you the night before a test because you rocked that subject. She's the coworker who was so much fun but "forgot" to put your name on the report you did together. She's the new gal in the neighborhood who was nice to you at the school fundraiser, then told everyone you had a drinking problem.

We're never 100 percent sure about the frenemy. She keeps us off balance by definition, and only time will out her as an enemy, since she usually starts off as a friend.

TELLTALE TRAITS OF THE FRENEMY

You feel kind of crappy after seeing her.

She was sort of nice, but also kind of …mean? You question yourself, wondering if you're being too sensitive. If you ask her, she'll tell you that, yes, you're definitely being too sensitive.

She's condescending.
She *wants* there to be a power imbalance. In a true friendship, the two of you are equals. A frenemy wants you to feel insecure. She'll invite the bosses to her housewarming party, but she won't invite you, and excuse the slight by saying that she thought to help you avoid situations where you can't really excel. Take notice.

She's passive-aggressive.
Say she asks you to meet her at 7 p.m. for dinner, just the two of you. She then shows up at 7:30 with two friends you've never met, and all night, she makes sure you feel left out. Or, you introduce her to your lovely new partner (she's single) and suddenly she has a migraine and has to leave. You get a promotion, she never congratulates you.

She gossips about other people.
Hell yes. She *loves* gossip, and she feeds it to you. Don't be tricked into thinking she's just funny, or she's only telling you this because you're special and have a close, close bond. She's playing you. And she will absolutely gossip about you. It's a guarantee.

She loves drama. (See "Drama Mama," Chapter 6).
A frenemy loves to stir the pot. You've said you don't want to socialize with Elsbeth, because she's a racist and homophobe, and yet, there's Elsbeth at your frenemy's house the next time you visit. Your friend could've given you the head's up so you could bow out. She didn't. She *wants* to watch the friction. She feeds on it.

She has an unkind word for everyone.
"I'm sorry I can't make our date for drinks," she texts. "I'm stuck with this loser who doesn't have any other friends, and

she won't stop talking." Oh, hon, she's not stuck. She *wants* to be with that other person! She's pretending to be stuck so she doesn't have to take responsibility. Imagine what she's saying about you.

She insults you.

Usually, she insults you in front of other people—your bosses or colleagues or relatives—under the guise of a joke. If you call her on it, she'll deflect and say it was funny, or you misinterpreted it, or gosh, she's so sorry, you know how much she likes you, right? Don't believe her. She meant every word of that insult.

She won't take responsibility for her actions.

She claims she wanted to show up for you, but …you know, her job, her family, her chronic illness, her cat's chronic illness, your imagination. She is always blameless, and often she's a victim (see "Draped in Red Flags," Chapter 4).

She takes your ideas, then blames you if they don't work out.

Frenemies (like Attention Whores and Drama Mamas) are insecure. They are also often lazy, more intent on working a person than working the problem. "*Joss* was the one who said we'd come up with that. I really don't know anything about it." Your only choice is to keep clear boundaries and document everything that happens for when the blame game becomes a problem, because honey, it will.

She accuses you of having ulterior motives.

She does this because *she* has ulterior motives, and if she accuses you first, it goes on record. With a frenemy, everything is a competition. "I feel like you didn't want me to get the promotion" is code for "If you were up for a promotion, I wouldn't want you to get it." People often accuse others of having their own motives. It's called projection. The competitive person accuses you of being competitive, even when you've never shown a shred of that behavior. The cheater accuses you of cheating. They truly don't understand that there is another way to be other than the way they are.

Your purpose is to make her look better.
All roads lead back to one thing: your frenemy is using you. When you are not benefiting her, you are worth nothing to her. If you're not helping her, she's unavailable to you. Kristan was in a frenemyship (which she thought was a friendship) that ended when she told her friend Bitter Betty —not her real name—that she could no longer help Betty with her work projects. Still, Kristan hoped to do other things with Betty, and said so. Just nothing work related. Betty dropped her like an anvil. Frenemies are users. Period.

Social Media Frenemies
Social media is fraught with competition and wretched behavior. The relative distance of virtual space make it easy for people to be nasty. Anyone can open a Twitter account and troll someone. Anyone can make a fake gmail account to post crappy reviews of someone's business. A person can get away with horrible behavior without having any accountability. Things that someone would *never* say to your face are gleefully posted online. Frenemies thrive here.

By now, we all know (hopefully) that Facebook and Instagram and TikTok videos aren't accurate depictions of reality. Most of us don't post about raw, upsetting events, dark moods, sulky reactions. We don't post pictures of our filthy bathrooms and write about how we binge-ate two boxes of Kraft dinners at 1 a.m. We don't post unflattering photos of ourselves (although Kristan is fond of posting bad hair pictures). We all know enough to take a grain of salt about how fabulously perfect everyone's life can look online.

Most of us use social media to share the highlights and funny events of our actual life. Joss posted most entertainingly when her dog got skunked; Kristan posted a picture of her daughter in scrubs when she graduated from nursing school. Frenemies, on the other hand, use social media to *benefit* themselves. Pay attention to what your frenemy says online, about herself, you *and* others. They are relentless self-praisers— "Just finished a project in a day when it took all my coworkers a week. Guess I'm on fire!"—or masters of the humble-brag. "Well, I didn't TELL my husband to buy me a $25,000 ring, and I'm mortified that I have to wear it, but I can't hurt his feelings, LOL!"

Also, watch what your frenemies ignore when you're wondering if this is a true friend or not. A frenemy will "miss" your good news and feign ignorance. "You got engaged? I didn't know!" is her way of saying, "You're not *important* enough for me to notice."

A frenemy may vague-book, too, posting about unnamed friends who used to be friends, to try to get sympathy. She wants *you* to think you're that crappy friend. She *wants* you to be on edge about the relationship. And you can bet she won't come clean if you ask her outright what she's talking about.

Another way frenemies try to deflect from your success is to respond to your happy news by announcing a tragedy.

You post:
Got into my top-choice law school! I'm so happy and excited!

She posts, minutes later:
Mr. Fluffers, my tiny kitten, is very sick. I won't be online for a while.

Dozens, maybe hundreds of people send their thoughts and prayers to Mr. Fluffers. She is grateful for their kindness. You message her, asking about Mr. Fluffers. She ignores you. You call. You go to voicemail. You follow up later in the week. Nothing. Then you read that Mr. Fluffers is miraculously better. She thanks everyone but you for the good wishes. And she sure as hell never mentions your acceptance into law school.

One of our listeners wrote that she sent flowers to a frenemy who was undergoing surgery. The patient posted pictures of every arrangement she got …except that one. Such are the habits of a frenemy.

Another common trait of frenemies is backstabbing. The frenemy posts this: *Had the most amaze-balls time with my gals last night! Are we great dancers? Hell YES, bitches! #BFFs #margaritas #mostfunever #tacosaremylife*

But on Monday, she has nothing but nasty things to say about those women in her group. You wonder why she'd trash her friends. Well, it's because she doesn't *have* friends. They served a purpose on Saturday—fun. On Monday, however, they serve a different purpose: to make you to feel more special to her than those other friends—at least, for a while.

It's easy to think the frenemy is out to get you, specifically. It's usually not true. Frenemies will work *everyone*. They're really not capable of true friendship because they're so busy comparing their lives to everyone else's. A frenemy will move on from one person to another, claiming friendship, having lunch, texting and hanging out until that person is used up. After she's taken what she can get, she moves on.

And once you identify that pattern, you'll see it more and more.

The Aftermath

One of our listeners wrote to express her frustration and anger with herself for wasting so much time on a frenemy she thought was a real friend. By the time she to wrote us, she was over it—even though she thought it took way too much time. But she was mourning the friendship she thought she had, and it took *months* to let that go.

That's okay. Our listener was trusting and hopeful, and those aren't bad things to be. Hopefully, she learned to be more discerning and, in the future, she will vet people more thoroughly before letting them become so deeply embedded in her life.

Should you warn someone away from a frenemy? That question came from another listener who'd had a bad experience at work. She wanted to warn the newest person the frenemy was grooming, to tell her to watch her back, but she was conflicted on how it might reflect on her professionally. Would she seem jealous? Bitter? Petty?

A tough question. In the end, she kept her mouth shut. She decided it wasn't her business, and everyone has to learn their own lessons. You might *want* to save someone the time and energy and emotions you experienced, but honey, you can't. You do you.

Remember, you deserve to have the kind of friend you *are*. Spend your time, emotions and energy on people who will reciprocate, who have your back and who want nothing but the best for you.

...

Why Do We Put Up with Frenemies?

Frenemies make us feel important.

It's easy to think someone's interested in you because you're great, and that's as it should be. But a frenemy is only interested in you, your career, your challenges to create the impression of caring. *You're negotiating for a raise? What did you say? What did the boss say? Do you think you'll get it? You totally deserve it!* Don't be fooled into thinking she cares about your career. She's simply gathering intel for ways to get her own raise.

She might say, "You make it look so effortless. How do you do that?" What she really wants is to use your tactics to better her own work. But hey, she's not you. She won't be able to do what you do. Mariano Rivera, the great Yankees closer, showed every pitcher who asked how to throw his famous cutter. That didn't mean they could throw it. They aren't Mariano.

Be very, very careful about what you say to her. Frenemies want to know where your weak spots are. This is one of the reasons frenemies love gossip. If you admit you don't love your boss, oh, honey. She's going to tell the boss. When she gossips about others, it's to make you feel like *you* are her only true and special friend.

At first, she seems so *genuine*. We know. This is a curse of Insta-Friendship (see Chapter 3). You jump in without looking. She wants to know everything so she can use the information, either to bolster herself or to take you down a peg. Everything is fodder for her plans. "You seem anxious. Is something going on?" she might ask. How considerate of her to notice! Nah. It's not her concern. It's intel that will come back to bite you. *Serena has an anxiety problem. I thought you knew. Poor thing would crack under pressure if we asked her to handle the presentation.*

Sometimes, it's necessary to stay "friends."
You live on the same street. You work in the same department. She's married to your sister. Getting along with her is something you have to do. You might not trust her as far as you can throw her, but sometimes, you might have to share a meal. It's okay to play along. Just be smart. Pay attention.

The relationship is spicy.
You take a few shots across the bow, fire a few back. You both know you're competing for the same thing, and maybe it's kind of fun. If you're behind, a frenemy might be an incentive for you to try harder. If you're ahead in the game, maybe that makes you feel good about yourself. (But check yourself on that. Wouldn't you rather be the woman who lifts other women up, rather than tears them down?)

Frenemies can help you.
Many frenemies are work- or project-related. You *can* benefit from them sometimes. The trick is knowing when and being very judicious in your participation. Examine your own motives so you don't become a frenemy yourself.

Your frenemy is not all bad.
They're not simply called enemies, after all. The friend part of a frenemy can be fun. But sometimes, we excuse bad behavior for far too long because of those fun times. Enjoy the fun and be wary of her attempts to get her hooks in you and trip you up.

CHAPTER 8

PLAYING THE VICTIM CARD

WE LADIES GOT A LETTER FROM OUR LISTENER, STILL Married, whose friend was going through a divorce. She wrote that her friend Zephyra (not her real name) wasn't happily married. The handwriting had been on the wall for a long time, but things took a turn when Zephyra found out her husband was cheating. According to Still Married, after the divorce, Zephyra became fixated on her ex-husband—what he did, how he was—and obsessed over how much he had lost in tossing her over for another woman, how bad things were for her now, how much she hated him.

Still Married was supportive and kind and visited Zephyra with the requisite cheap Chardonnay. Divorce is a special kind of hell, and of course a person needs her friends. But after four years, Zephyra was still mad at her ex-huband, and Still Married was tired. Zephyra couldn't seem to let go of the old wound. All roads led back to her divorce, despite the fact that Zephyra had found someone new, worked at a job she loved and had bought a darling house. Those positive things didn't seem to matter. Whenever Still Married mentioned a happy time spent with her own husband—an anniversary trip or a movie they had seen—Zephyra's eyes would fill, and Still Married would feel guilty for mentioning her coupledom.

Still Married ended her letter saying she was worn out by Zephyra's "divorce obsession," and by the anger and misery Z just couldn't seem to get past. Should she talk to Zephyra and tell her how she felt? Would Zephyra even care?

We didn't think it was wrong for Still Married to want Zephyra to be more self-aware. Zephyra was getting a lot from her friend—constantly bringing conversations back to herself, needing constant support and comforting—and seemed to give very little.

This behavior is what we Ladies call "playing the victim card."

Your friend is a good person, you think. She has many good qualities, so she's not a toxic friend in the traditional sense. She's not *mean*. In fact, she's quite nice—but, according to her, she's had the worst luck in the *universe*: horrible childhood, wretched relationships, accidents, bad jobs, bad friends, bad romance, bad family.

There's a pattern there. When someone views herself as the passive recipient of shitty luck—always—it's not a coincidence. Everyone has trials and tribulations to handle, and, sure, some people have more than others. Sometimes, these trials are out of our control—a tree falling on our house, or being diagnosed with cancer. But how we deal with our past trials and present difficulties says a lot about our character.

Some people have had terrible trauma in their lives and still go on to live very happy, positive lives. Some people are dealing with absolutely wretched situations and still laugh and smile. Life is what you make it, and these folks have chosen to make it happy.

The Victim Card Friend does the opposite.

Please note, we're not talking about people who have

truly been victimized by circumstances like the death of a loved one, illness, assault, violence. No. We're talking about a person who considers herself a victim for reasons that have very little to do with real-life events.

What Is a Victim Card Friend?

The VCF fails to take responsibility for the events and people in her life.

Rather than believing that she has the power to make changes and create good relationships, the VCF feels the Universe is against her. Not only is her glass half-empty, it's cracked, leaking and, whoops, someone just broke it. She is *not* a survivor who has gotten through or is getting through a difficult time. She is in its grip, now and forever more.

The VCF feels tremendously sorry for herself.

According to the VCF, something is *always* wrong. She is rarely upbeat and excited—she's depressed, melancholy, sick, stressed, overtired. That snowstorm feels *very* personal, and of *course* it happened the day she was traveling. It's just the way her life goes, she says. It never fails.

The VCF compares herself to others and always winds up the loser.

Her glass is broken. *Your* glass is beautiful. Of course, you got the perfect glass. She always gets the broken one. Did you see everyone else's glasses? Not a crack to be seen. Except for hers. And so on.

There's a weird power play in always painting yourself as the loser. It's a manipulative act designed to get your friends to reassure you that you're amazing, wonderful, strong and brilliant. The act gets you more help, more attention, more time. The VCF requires that her friends compliment and bolster her—a lot.

The VCF is passive, unable to speak or act for herself while dealing with her problems.

You've probably heard her say something like, "I wanted to say to him, 'You can't speak to me that way.'" To which you might reply, "Why *didn't* you?" To which she might likely say, "I couldn't" or "Maybe next time I will" or "That would've been impossible" or "I wish I had" or "If only you'd been there, you could've said it for me."

Hint: The VCF will never stand up for herself. And she is very comfortable being shat upon. If God or the Universe or Life is causing these things, it's not her fault, is it? It was preordained. She has an excuse for every time she picked the wrong person to love, accepted the crap job, didn't speak up to her boss, was misdiagnosed by the doctor. The world is out to get her.

Everything supports the idea that she is the Victim.

Dr. Khaleesi, a friend of our podcast and a real-life psychologist, tells us that victims globalize small events that support their claim. In other words, everything that happens goes into the evidence bag that supports her identity as Bad Luck Sally, even if it's something small, like stepping in dog poo. We've all stepped in dog poo, but the VCF views it as a personal message from the Universe, telling her that she *is* the dog poo. A non-Victim would simply tell the dog owner, "Clean up after your damn dog!"

· · ·

The VCF's issue has all the power.

Say your Victim has multiple sclerosis. She might say, "I can't go on that roller coaster, because I have multiple sclerosis." If you point out that other people (perhaps even you) have multiple sclerosis and still go on roller coasters, she will have an excuse. In her particular case, she will explain, there is a complication, and for her roller coasters are out forever. End of discussion.

Maybe it's true that her condition is complicated, but the VCF will whip out that card a lot. She may also make herself a spokesperson: "People with MS can't . . ." has more power than "*I* can't." Playing that role puts her in a large group of other (perhaps fictional) people who, she can claim, feel the same way she does. It keeps her issue front and center and also makes the idea she is fragile more believable. If she had simply said, "I don't like roller coasters," that would have been her *choice*. The VCF doesn't like having choices. They *like* to be victims. It's a comfy position and excuses them from personal responsibility.

The VCF finds no fault with herself.

The VCF feels that, if only the *Thing*—the illness, accident, childhood, horrible spouse—had not happened, life would be utterly perfect. Why? Because the VCF is the smartest, best, hardest working, kindest person in the *world*. It's only that *Thing*, or that series of Things, that have held her back.

Again, note the lack of responsibility. If X hadn't happened, your friend would by now be POTUS or a skilled surgeon, or would live in a huge house overlooking the Pacific and be Oprah's best friend, if not Oprah herself—or all of the above.

Tragically, the Thing or Things did occur, through no

fault of her own. Her parents are unsupportive, her sister is jealous, her boss is evil, her husband is wimpy, her child is sick. She never acknowledges her own limitations …because if she did, she would have to own up to the fact that she *isn't* Oprah.

Interestingly, only the VCF paints herself with superlatives. Her mother might roll her eyes at her, her kids would probably describe her differently. If anyone questions her view that she is the best person ever, she'll react with hurt. How *painful* it is to be overlooked! Then again, she'll say, she's used to it.

The VCF will not take action to address whatever is making her feel like a Victim.

There may be help out there, but she doesn't want it. Her problem defines her. She needs it! You (you fool) may genuinely want to help your friend. You offer advice, but there's always a reason she can't take it. She doesn't have enough time, money, energy. Her job is overwhelming. Too many people need her. Actually, she tried that already and it didn't work. Reasons. So many reasons.

The VCF will accept—and frequently request—favors, however. You might not be able to solve her issues for her (you can't, in fact, and it's not your job) but you can clean out her basement for her. If you're too busy to help, she will become wounded, sad, lonely, maybe a little tragic. She is owed, you see, because of the Thing that happened to her.

The VCF will not help.

You might think a VCF would be a sympathetic and helpful friend, but she is not. *She* is the victim here, not you. If you're going through something difficult, she's not going to show up at your door. She would, of course. She says she wants to, but she's too busy. Unlike you, she has that Victim Card to play …every time. Her role is to receive, not to give.

The VCF is short on genuine sympathy.

Your VCF might listen to your woes and say, "Gosh, I'm sorry." But really, she's weighing your issue. If she deems it not as important as yours, that's all you'll get—lip service. Inevitably, the conversation swings back to her. She always has it worse. That's her identity, remember? *She's* Bad Luck Sally. Not you.

She may say something like, "I *wish* I had those kinds of problems!" or "Be grateful you *have* a partner!" and the like. She delegitimizes your issues because, in her heart of hearts, she believes you're just not as important as she is.

The VCF will drop you if you fail to show up on command.

In her eyes, your job is to be there for her. If you tire, if you get frustrated with her constant Victimhood, you're out. She'll talk to other friends about how you failed her. She'll say not everyone can be friends with someone who's dealing with…the Thing (note the dodged responsibility: it's her Thing, not her). But that's the challenge you accepted when you became friends with her. Your role is to believe her, be there for her, do for her. Once you step out of that role, you become the crappy friend. At least, that's what she'll think and say. In reality, you're simply establishing boundaries and setting a limit on how much of your time and energy you give to her.

· · ·

Why is She Like This?

We Ladies don't know for sure. We can guess that underneath all her self-identified sainthood, suffering and martyrdom is a deep fear of failure and insecurity. The Thing that made her the victim? It is, she wrongly thinks, the most interesting thing that ever happened to her. She gets more attention because of it. She can always be in a special group: women who've been cheated on, sexual assault survivor, abused child, person suffering from a chronic illness, person who survived a terrible car wreck, etc..

Her Thing is real. It happened. But most people don't create their entire identity around an illness or tragic event. Whatever happened shaped them in *some* way, of course, but it's not their entire story. For the VCF, it is her entire story.

We Ladies know two women who grew up in abject poverty. They lived through incredibly difficult situations no child should endure, and that absolutely leaves marks.

Our first friend—let's call her Fabulosa—reacted to her childhood poverty by becoming very financially secure. She loves her possessions, loves to shop, and UPS is at her house almost daily. "I grew up really poor," she told Kristan one night as they were at her lovely home. "So being able to buy this new couch means the world to me."

What a natural, healthy response to a very difficult childhood! Fabulosa is actively creating what she didn't have as a kid: a comfortable home, plenty of clothes, plenty of security. Does she go too far with the shopping sometimes? Sure! So what? She can afford it. Shopping makes her happy. She's proud of surviving her early difficulties, but she doesn't roll around in them. Growing up in poverty was something that happened to her. It's not who she is.

Our second friend—let's call her Weary-Anna—talks about her difficult childhood every time we get together. She keeps the heat in her house set painfully low. She didn't have heat as a kid because they were poor. She can't join you for a drink, because she grew up poor, and wine was a luxury her family couldn't afford. Weary-Anna admires your sweater, but could never spend so much on a cashmere sweater, because she grew up poor. (You may have gotten the sweater as a gift. It may be polyester. It may have cost forty-seven cents at Savers. It doesn't matter.)

Weary-Anna drags her childhood along as *the* defining incident of her life. Her kids, her job, her partner, her education, her gorgeous singing voice—nothing matters nearly as much as that childhood.

So that's our VCF. Now, what about yours? Did she pick you because you're a mush and never fail to give her the time and space and shoulder to cry on that she needs? Yes, my lamb, she did. Of course, you're wonderful for being a good friend to her, but mostly, you'll have to *do* for her. You've volunteered to be sucked in by this black hole of need. You'll never have enough time and sympathy for her, and even though you really prefer a more reciprocal friendship, there you are, sitting beside her on her couch again, listening to her latest injustice. Why do you buy in?

Let's assume your VCF has enough good qualities that you want to stay friends (or have to, because she's linked to you somehow outside of friendship …work, family, etc.). How can you stay in but still bow out of the drama?

Why You Buy In and How to Bow Out

You don't want to seem mean.

Sigh. There it is again, that irritating "don't want to be mean" bullshit. Still, we Ladies understand. We've been there. Women are conditioned to be *nice*, to put others first, and sweetheart, let's get over that. This person is not your child, and you are not a saint. Friendship should have balance. Of *course* you should be there when a friend needs you, but she should be there for you, too. You deserve that. You get to ask for that. If you think you can't do that with your friend, she's not really a friend.

Speak the truth: Make a private date with her one day and tell her how you feel. *I feel like I'm always here for you, but you're not here for me.* Let that statement sit a minute. Let her address it. Her response will tell you a lot about whether your friendship can grow.

You have a better life than hers, and helping her seems the least you can do.

Oh, my God, what a ridiculous thing to say (but Kristan has said it herself, too). You're allowed to have a good life and not feel guilty about it. You've *made* your life good. That was not an accident.

This line of thought devalues your time and energy. Is it really your job to listen to the VCF's list of the ways God/the Universe/Life have kicked her in the proverbial nutsack? No. It's not. You're not her therapist.

Give her only as much time and energy as you want to spare: Be specific. For example, say, "I'm free for half an hour this week, but after that, the month gets really busy. Would you like to meet Thursday at ten for a quick cup of coffee?"

She really does have problems.

Again, her problems are not yours to fix—and you lack the superpower to fix them even if you wanted to. Don't be manipulated by her just because things are hard for her. A non-Victim Card Friend goes through a hard time and *comes out of it* (see Fabulosa, above). That type of friend accepts your help and appreciates your time and empathy. She does not demand it. The VCF will *never* come out of it, and you're trying to fill the ocean with an eyedropper. In other words, you'll never be done giving.

Turn the solution back on her, rather than trying to solve her problem yourself: Dr. Khaleesi, our psychologist pal, gave us the following suggestion: When your VCF mentions her struggles, say, "That sounds hard. What's your plan?" Just saying those words let her know that you've listened, and that you're interested in hearing what she will *do for herself.* No swooping in to save the day, missy. You've done enough of that, and you always hit your head on the wall, don't you? You're only responsible for your own life, and you're incapable of fixing someone else's.

There's a world of difference between a VCF and a friend who's going through a hard time. We *all* go through hard times. We all need our friends a certain points in our lives. But if your friend makes you tired, depressed, irritated, furious, do you have to stay with her? No. That's not friendship, sweetheart. That's exploitation, and the kind of exploitation in which you are a willing partner. You deserve better.

CHAPTER 9

GOSSIP AND SECRETS

GOSSIP, NOUN.

Casual or unconstrained conversation or reports about other people, typically involving details that are not confirmed as being true

—Lexico

For many people, gossip is as delicious as chocolate. We Ladies know and accept this. By definition, gossip is inflammatory, naughty and in many cases, lurid. *Ooh! Did you hear about Lucretia? She got fired for day-drinking at the hospital!*

To be clear, gossip is spread out of malice. It's *not* one friend asking another friend's advice about Lucretia, who may have a drinking problem. It's the spreading of unconfirmed details that make someone else look bad.

Friends talk about each other. Female friends especially. That's not always bad—not at all! Kristan might say to Joss, "Yara and I spent four hours on the phone the other night!" to which Joss would likely say, "Oh, my God, I love that woman." This is not gossip. This is sharing the love. Joss might say to Kristan, "I'm worried about Yara. I think she's doing too much these days. She just got out of the hospital!" That's mutual concern. But gossip …gossip has that hint of excitement and secrecy and rumor to it. *I heard that Yara showed Ernie her boobs so he'd give her free pizza! Can you believe it?*

Gossip is seductive. It's so easy to get caught up in something that, ultimately, has nothing to do with you, especially when the drama is so juicy. When Gossipéna calls you, announcing she has tea to spill, and you are the very first person she called …well, hell, it's both thrilling and flattering. There is *news*, and *you* are the one to be trusted with it. Let the tea flow!

Welp, here's what might happen. Gossipéna tells you that Apollonia's husband has been cheating on her! AND the other woman is—wait for it—your other friend, Sluttiara! Girrrlll, Sluttiara is ready to move in with him, the skank, and Apollonia has NO IDEA! He's waiting till after Baby Girl's First Communion to drop the bomb.

OMG, so much to unpack.

First, this news is both shocking and thrilling. It's a soap opera come to life! So much more interesting than swapping tips on how to get wine stains out of clothing.

Second, Apollonia is your best homegirl. Her husband is screwing your other homegirl.

Do you tell her? It may feel like the answer is "yes, definitely." *That's my best friend and she deserves to know, and I'm not going to let her bring that asshole to her parents' house for a First Communion party, knowing he's cheating on her!* But you also know that life's just not that black and white. Marriage is complicated, and do you really want to be the one to explode your friend's life? Except he's cheating, you say, and *someone's* gonna tell her. Shouldn't it be you?

Third. Okay, so you know. You found out secondhand,

but you *know*. Do you tell your friend that you know and be like, "I knew he wasn't shit at your damn rehearsal dinner?" Or do you wait for her to tell you? And if you wait, does that mean you don't care?

Fourth. *Everybody* now knows that Apollonia's husband cheated, but they also know that your friend stopped having sex with her husband months ago. She's been a super bitch to everyone, especially to her husband, and they know because Apollonia hasn't been shy about sharing at book club. Might Apollonia be happy about this affair? Relieved?

Fifth. Apollonia may well know her husband is cheating with her friend already. Give the woman some credit.

Finally, and most important, you ache for your friend, no matter what. People are talking about her problems, and those problems are significant. Her life has become a maelstrom, and you wish you had a way to lead her to a calm oasis.

This kind of situation is murky for all involved, with potential pitfalls everywhere.

So do you speak up or butt out? What the hell *is* your role here?

Speak Up or Butt Out?

Opt out of gossip.

As delicious as the he-said-she-said gossip may be, if your friend is a major player in the drama, remove yourself from that discussion. Be brief. A "Hey ladies, can we change the subject?" should do the trick. If that doesn't work, don't be afraid to be blunt: "Stop. She's my friend, and I'm not comfortable with this conversation."

These statements should make your position clear—you're Team Bestie all the way. When you contribute to speculation, even in a small way, you are giving fuel to the gossip, and that can only lead to more pain for your friend. You'd want her to stand up for you, right? So be that stand-up person.

Should you be the one to tell her?

Hey, Apollonia, I just got back from margaritas with the girls, and rumor has it your boo is sleeping with Sluttaria.

Oh, girl. Most women *say* they would want to know, but there are factors that you should take into consideration before you spill. Ask yourself a couple of questions first.

Am I one of her BFFs, with a track record of good communication and support through good times and bad? Or are you more of a friend because of shared history rather than true intimacy? Make a serious and thorough analysis of your friendship. Don't just assume you are the bestest of friends because she was a bridesmaid in your wedding fifteen years ago, or even because you grew up together. If your revelation has the potential to change your friend's life for the worse, make sure your friendship has the foundation to survive the storm.

Am I directly involved? This means, did you witness something with your own eyes? Did you run into your bestie's husband with his fling just as they were unclutching from a romantic embrace? Did you lock eyes with him in a way he knows he was busted? If so, we Ladies feel you are under no obligation to keep secrets for someone being so open about their duplicity. You can always say to him, "You tell her or I will."

Maybe you just heard the news from a colleague who knows someone who said she met Sluttaria at a work event, where she was all over your friend's husband. If you think you're going to begin a discussion with your bestie with the words, "I heard from a friend of a friend...." it's not your place to get involved.

Don't be judgy. Now is not the time.

If your friend's behavior contributed to the shit storm gathering on the horizon, now is not the time to bring that up. Telling your friend that her husband is a louse and then following that up with, "but you haven't exactly been a princess either" won't end well. Neither will showing solidarity by saying you never liked her husband anyway. It may *seem* like you're being a great friend, but disparaging her husband, no matter how dreadful he is, disparages her choice of him. Do you really want to imply in any way that your buddy was stupid for choosing such a loser? (The answer is no, just in case there is any doubt.)

If you are compelled to say something, be very careful how you say it.

If you're an eyewitness to the event that started the gossip —that is, if you saw the husband with Sluttaria—pick a good time to talk with Apollonia, just the two of you when you won't be interrupted. Ask her how things are on the home front. Let her be the one to bring up the issue first. Maybe she'll open up to you, and she'll never have to know she has been the topic of discussion over margaritas.

Remember, if you're the one to drop this bomb—if Apollonia really is in the dark—she'll never forget that you were the one to tell her. That fact carries emotional baggage no matter how well intentioned you are. For both of you.

When Kristan was in middle school, her teacher called a meeting of all the girls in the class, except Hydrangea (not her real name). The subject of the conversation was

Hydrangea's personal hygiene and body odor. The teacher (who should've found a different field more suited to her nature—prison matron, for example) thought one of the girls should tell Hydrangea.

Guess who was chosen?

Kristan sat down after school the next day, per the teacher's orders, and, as gently as possible, told Hydrangea she didn't smell so good and needed to shower more often. Hydrangea burst into tears. Kristan felt two inches tall.

Years later, Hydrangea is an extraordinarily successful person with many advanced degrees, a family, a great reputation. Yet whenever Kristan runs into her, she feels ashamed. She caused this lovely person embarrassment and pain at a tender age. Even at twelve years old, Kristan knew the teacher's suggestion was not kind. To this day, she hates that teacher. To this day, she's sorry to have hurt Hydrangea.

So. Telling. It's fraught. For both of you. Your friend will forever remember who gave her the bad news…and you'll always remember that you spoke the sentence that sliced open her heart.

If you decide you must speak up, first ask Apollonia if it's alright to bring up a difficult subject. *I have something really uncomfortable to discuss. It's about your husband. Is it okay if I continue?* If she says yes, be concise and stick to the facts. *I was at Señor Gaucho's for Taco Tuesday last week, and I saw your husband kissing Sluttaria. I'm sure it was them.*

From that sentence on, let your friend drive the conversation. You have given her the facts. She may know them already, she may not care, she may be devastated. No matter what reaction she has, be supportive. If she's destroyed, give her a hug, tell her you're there for her and suggest therapy to get her through this tough time. Bad news can be borne in a much healthier way if a skilled professional is guiding you through the process.

. . .

The Gossipers

We Ladies cannot stress this enough: If a friend calls you to gossip about another friend, she is also gossiping about you. You are not immune. You're not! You think, yeah, well, she's my *best friend*, and she'd never gossip about *me*. Wrong. She's *already* gossiping about you. Trust us.

People who gossip do so because it makes them feel powerful. They have the news, the rumor, they're the ones who are so connected that nothing happens without their knowing it. Dishing gossip is both a way to show superiority ("I know this and you don't!") and also a way to degrade the subject of this gossip ("She's such a slut/cheater/drunk!").

Gossips often target people who make them feel insecure. Say Joss's neighbor wants to have Joss as her new best friend (Joss gets this *constantly*). The neighbor sees that Kristan is always visiting Joss, or they're always doing something together. But *she* wants to be the bestie! So she says to Joss, "You know, that Kristan …I know she's your best friend, but did you see her the other day as she left your house? She gave me such a mean look! It was like she was warning me away from you. Weird."

By throwing shade on Kristan, the neighbor is hoping to worm her way closer to Joss. Bitch, back off. First of all, Joss can make friends with whomever she chooses. If she wants you as a friend, you'll know. Second, do you really think Joss is dumb enough to fall for that game? She's not. And third, friendship should never be a competition. We can all have as many best friends as we like.

One of our listeners, Rainbow Mom, wrote that she was very, very close friends with Nickel—not her real name. As described, Nickel seemed like a wonderful, generous friend who loved entertaining in her big, beautiful home, having friends to her summer house, inviting our letter writer to the occasional concert or splashy event. They were, it seemed, best friends. But Nickel always had something bad to say about someone else. She'd call up Rainbow Mom and say, "Hey, we were having dinner with the Calloways the other night. She made a joke about gays. And your kid is gay. I thought you should know."

Well…chances are good that the mother of a gay kid can spot homophobia from a mile away. But whatever. Nickel is just being loyal—right? But the next time Rainbow Mom was invited to Nickel's house, guess who else was there? The homophobic Ms. Calloway.

Was Nickel trying to mediate between her homophobic friend and the parent of a gay kid? Hell, no! She wanted to watch the friction.

Why? Because Nickel loves drama. It's how she makes her life interesting. She was stirring the pot, then throwing in some gasoline. As time passed, Rainbow Mom began to see a pattern. Nickel always had something negative to say about someone, especially her own friends. At first, Rainbow Mom felt…special. Nickel was telling *her* about these other, lesser friends, right? So that was just proof of how *different* her relationship with Nickel was. Right?

Wrong.

You know how this ends. Rainbow Mom finally called Nickel on her behavior, and Nickel stabbed her in the back so fast Rainbow barely saw the knife. It wasn't a surprise, but it still sliced deep.

It was just a matter of time. The Nickels of the world are not worth two cents. Good riddance to bad rubbish, the Ladies said.

Gossips are not going to be good friends. Are they all evil? No, not necessarily. Just watch your back. Let them know you don't engage in or approve of gossip. You don't have to flounce off and slam the door—just shut it down and keep it that way. Your reputation as a person of integrity will shine.

Are You a Gossiper?

Does talking about your friends with friends make you a gossip? Girl, no. We're women. We like to analyze personalities and people and talk about issues and troubles and everything under the sun. There's absolutely nothing wrong with talking about one friend with another if you're concerned, shocked or even aggravated. The difference between gossip and, say, venting, is love.

Say three of you are friends, and one friend continues to bang her head against the brick wall of a crappy marriage. Year after year, you hear the same complaints. She doesn't love her husband. He's not a nice person. She wants to divorce him but won't. She tells you the same stories that always have the same results and yet she won't take action to make a change.

You are allowed to call your mutual friend to complain. *Why doesn't she leave him? God! How many more years of her life will she waste! I can't stand hearing this anymore!*

You are venting out of frustration, yes, but also out of love. You know you're not going to fix her problems for her, and your mutual friend knows the same thing. You both understand that, sometimes, you just have to vent.

In this case, your feelings are justified and come from a place of caring, and your conversation is safe with your mutual friend. How do you know this? Because you've been true friends for a long time. She has integrity. And that's not just what you think about her. It's clear from how she lives.

· · ·

Knowing Secrets

Yara, a close friend of both Ladies, visited the podcast to discuss the power of secrets, and how telling them—and knowing them—can erode a friendship.

Yara makes friends easily. She has a big heart, gives lots of time and energy to people and to her causes. She loves to entertain and has a gift for making everyone feel special. Small wonder that she befriended Avocado—not her real name (obviously).

It seemed Avocado was living her best life—the mother of two small children, madly in love with her husband, working for herself, close pals with her mom. An easy, fun friendship began between Yara and Avocado, until one day, Avocado confided all to Yara.

Yara's husband was cheating on her with a high school flame. Not only that, he was saying and doing all the most unforgivable things spouses can say and do to each other. *I've never known what love was until now. I finally get what all the fuss is about sex. I never loved you.* He lied, he snuck around, he had his lover move into their neighborhood. He gave Avocado an STD.

She kicked him out. She changed the locks and confided her agonizing heartbreak to Yara. There were so many phone calls. She received so much love and support, the kind that Yara is known for.

And then ...the skanky-ass husband came back. Seemed his new love was cheating on him. Could he come home?

Avocado said yes.

When she told Yara about her decision, Yara answered very carefully. "I hope you get all the happiness you deserve." Did Yara think this husband was truly sorry? Of course not. Did she think a happy marriage lay ahead? No. But she cared about her friend and respected her decision as much as she could because, Avocado told her, "I still love him." Yeah, okay, whatever. But Yara was not about to abandon her friend.

Except Avocado abandoned *her*. Completely. Totally. Unfriended her on social media, blocked her number—the whole nine yards. For two years, Yara had been an unwavering support, in Avocado's corner, unflinchingly loyal no matter what the woman decided. But now that Avocado was back pretending to be happy on Facebook and talking about what a great guy her husband was, Yara's services were no longer needed.

Yara knew too much. She knew everything, every mortifying length Avocado went to in the beginning to keep her skanky-ass husband, every hurt he inflicted on her, the cruel words he said, the screamingly obvious fact that Avocado was still not his first choice. The punishment for this loyalty—and this knowledge—was to cut Yara out of Avocado's life completely. Yara was stunned. She'd never judged Avocado for taking back the skanky-ass husband. She truly wanted what was best for her.

We Ladies suggested to Yara that Avocado might be ashamed—in her heart, she likely knew she was too weak or scared to be alone, knew that her husband had no honor and that their marriage going forward would be a sham. But, for her, being in a sham marriage was better than being single. We Ladies surmised that every time Avocado saw Yara, she also had to see herself through Yara's lens—as the woman who had been gutted by her cheating, disease-riddled, cruel husband …and was overjoyed to have him back. Some people can't live with their secrets being out there.

Marriage is so personal. Yara understands this, but the hurt remained. To be ghosted by a friend after you've been nothing but *wonderful* is wrenching. It took time to get over the pain, but the lesson was learned.

Many friendships will run into tests because of gossip

and secrets. What to do when our morals clash with a situation in our friend's life? Would you want to be friends with this person, knowing what you do? Are you willing to watch them flail with the same problem year after year without doing anything to eradicate that problem? Answer these questions to take stock of your relationship. Knowing if you are on solid ground will help you decide when to speak up and when to butt out.

CHAPTER 10

THE FRIENDSHIP
BALANCING ACT

WE LADIES, BEST FRIENDS FOREVER, ARE VERY different in how much time we each spend with friends. Kristan, whose coworkers are of the four-legged variety because she works at home, doesn't go a week without seeing a friend or six (unless she's under house arrest for various reasons). She arranges nights out, occasionally hosts gatherings, invites friends to go away for weekends, asks them to her house for coffee or wine. She's an empty nester, so the idea of having people in her house is exciting. She loves her solitude, but she loves company, too.

Joss, on the other hand, works with humans at her day job and cherishes long stretches of solitude. She's usually *not* the person to send out a text asking when four pals can get together and then makes the reservation. She's the person who responds to text invitations from Kristan and others— usually with a yes, occasionally with a no. Every year or so, she invites her friends to her house, but entertaining isn't really her gig. That being said, she's an excellent guest, happy to come over for a fancy dinner or popcorn and cheap Chardonnay. Likewise, if you call her up and ask if you can hang at your place, the answer is probably yes ...unless she's busy, tired, cooking, reading in bed or deeply involved in a Jason Bateman marathon.

Neither way of being is wrong. We two—extrovert and introvert—are still besties. We talk via email and text and phone almost daily and see each other once or twice a month. A couple of times a year, we go away for the weekend together. Laughter and shenanigans ensue. But friendship requires balance. We all need friends, but our needs vary. A text every month might suffice for one friendship. A text an hour might be the norm for another. There's a difference between need and needy (see Chapters 4, 6 ...and 8!). Iphegenia (Chapter 4) was a needy friend. She was constantly texting, emailing, making plans, extending invitations, dropping in. Nothing wrong with enjoying one's pals. But needing them to fill some kind of emptiness—well, that's different.

Iphigenia craved the validation of friendship. Maybe she felt that if she wasn't constantly in our faces, we'd forget about her, which says a lot about her self-esteem. She didn't enjoy solitude, ever. Was she avoiding deeper problems? Maybe. We're not shrinks, but it does seem that a person who can't be alone is dodging some uncomfortable thoughts.

One of our listeners wrote about a friend who was friend-obsessed, and yet was not great company when they did get together. She turned each conversation into a discussion of her obsession with celebrities. The letter writer didn't know how to create a healthy distance with her friend and had trouble directing the conversation to something other than The Real Housewives.

We Ladies suggested the letter writer have a frank conversation with her friend—admit that there are limits on her time and energy, that she lacks interest in the Kardashians, and would like to get together less frequently and do things that require more than conversation—bowling, for example, or paint night.

Mindy Kaling brilliantly wrote the book *Is Everyone Hanging Out Without Me?* to talk about the fear of missing out. With so much social media, it's too easy to ruin an otherwise wonderful night on your own by checking a feed and spotting a photo of your friends clubbing or eating out together. You get a sick feeling in your stomach. *Am I not wanted? Doesn't she like me as much as she used to? Do I like her more than she likes me? Am I a crappy friend?*

So many of our listeners write to tell us they suffer from fear of missing out and are hurt by not being invited to gatherings. They wonder why *they* are always the ones who have to initiate plans to be included.

Listen, chickadee. People are allowed to hang out together without you. Different friends serve different purposes. If you want a quiet, intimate lunch to talk about books, maybe Christine is your go-to pal. If you want to toss back a couple drinks and rock the karaoke machine, Priscilla and Julie are your girls.

Your friends get to make the same choices. You don't have to be included all the time. If you want to make a pain in the ass of yourself, take it personally. Tell your friend how hurt you were not to be included. *Why didn't you invite me? I'm crushed! I cried all night!*

She had some reason for not inviting you (as you may well have a reason for not inviting her to everything). She doesn't owe you every minute of her social life. If you've given her every minute of yours, always including her in everything you do, well, sweetheart, that's your choice. (But the Ladies will be so bold as to suggest that, if you stop and think about it, that is probably *not* always the case.)

Different friends for different reasons and seasons. When you're the one making the plans, consider who fits best for what. You want to see a movie? Host a group dinner? Go rollerblading in the park? Chat at 3:00 a.m.? Not every friend is going to want to do those things.

And even if you do "invite her to everything, damn it!" she does not have to reciprocate in kind. Friendship is a gift, not a debt to be paid. If the scales are so far out of balance in your friendship, it could well be that she's saying she's just not that into you. We're sorry. That's hard, and we've been through it, too.

Now, if you believe a friend *is* excluding you to send a message, it's time to put on those big-girl panties and ask her to lunch. Chat for a while. Be pleasant. Say how nice it is to see her. Then go ahead and mention your concern. *Is everything okay between us? I noticed that you had the gang over for First Friday Fajitas and didn't invite me. I hope you know if you're upset with me, you can talk about it.*

Then *listen.* Don't deny her feelings and experience. She's your *friend.* You like her and care about how she feels. Think before you respond. There's a difference to expressing how you feel and telling someone off. When it's your turn to speak, don't make it all about you. Don't accuse her of being a bad or thoughtless friend. Phrases such as, "I hear you," or "I can see your side of it," and "That makes sense" show that you're truly considering her side of things. Remember the "when you do X, I feel Y" way of presenting your feelings.

Be honest. Tell her if you felt a little left out or confused. Then listen. Listen. *Listen.* It's a cornerstone of friendship and humanity. People who listen to others are kinder, more compassionate, smarter, more fun to be around. Be one of those people.

Having a few close friends is wonderful. Having a large group of friends is also wonderful. Having one soul-sister who'll hold your hand as you're dying—wonderful. Friendship comes in many different shapes and sizes. Don't try to squeeze one person into every role.

Like flowers in a garden (gag, but yeah), friendships need a little breathing room to grow and flourish. Don't feel that your every spare moment has to be spent with someone else. You can find so much joy and insight in solitude. Friends are important, but they shouldn't be everything to you. A well-rounded person has a happier life. Enjoy your down time, have hobbies. Take good care of you. Be an interesting person who explores new things and meets new people. Your life will be better for it.

The Many Types of Friends
There is, we Ladies believe, many types of friends. They may look something like this:

The true-blue friend: Time-tested, crisis-proved, you two are able to talk about your friendship—even when you're going through a rough patch. She will visit you in the hospital just to make you laugh. She spends her free time with you. She *wants* to. She listens. You talk and see each other often. You enjoy the same things. You could be sisters, the good kind.

The bestie best friend: She's a blast. You love her. You always have fun when you're together. But you two only see each other once in a while, and you're not privy to each other's inner lives and issues—which is A-okay. Enjoy those laughs and wild adventures and keep them coming.

The historic best friend: She's known you since forever. You have a history of shared experiences. Maybe, if you met today, you wouldn't choose each other, but that history is precious to you both. You are always comfortable with each other, even though your lives are now very different.

The circumstantial best friend: You're both on the same committee, you always sit together, you *love* this person … but life doesn't throw you together that often. Without that committee, there's not a lot to talk about, and that's fine. Not every friendship fits in every corner. You have a friend to sit next to during those meetings, someone who makes that time a lot more enjoyable. Enjoy away!

The fascinating best friend: There's a lot you two don't agree about, but those differences are interesting. You're highly sexual, she's celibate. She has ten children, you're childless by choice. You love cosmetic surgery, she's firmly against it. But you have *fun* together, and she challenges your brain, even if you think she's kind of whack (and she thinks the same thing about you).

The Jane Austenian best friend: You two have so much in common. There's never a cross word between you. You enjoy reading, embroidery and playing the pianoforte. And yet, maybe that's all there is—common interests and pleasant conversations. Don't sell this friendship short! You might not want to spend weeks at a time with her, so continue to just enjoy her in short bursts.

The work best friend: Every day, you have lunch together and talk about your coworkers, your work, your boss, your assistant. You look forward to going to work because she's there, and she's a blast. But outside of work, things sorta … peter out. Again, *fine.* Everyone needs an ally at work and having someone who brightens your 9-to-5 is a blessing.

The older-than-you friend: Significantly older. This person might've been your friend's mom growing up, or a teacher you had in school. The power balance might be skewed in this friendship, but the value is super high. Maybe she's the mother you wish you had, or is your work mentor, or is the kind of person you'd like to be when you're that age. Show her that you value her and pay attention to what she says.

The could've-been best friend: You *really* like and admire this person. You see each other here and there and know that, given the chance, yours could become a beautiful friendship. But it never does. Circumstances, timing or obligations conspire against it, so you two are limited to meeting at the odd school fundraiser, in a book club group or once a year at the town's street cleanup. For no good reason, your friendship just never took root. Maybe things will shift someday, and a deeper closeness will develop. If not, it's okay. It's still great to know someone you admire and enjoy.

CHAPTER 11

THE ART OF THE APOLOGY

IN OUR SOCIETY, MAKING APOLOGIES IS CONSIDERED A weakness. We Ladies firmly disagree.

We all screw up, say the wrong thing, fail to show up, deliberately or accidentally exclude someone. Those actions are hurtful, whether the hurt is big or little. NO ONE has gotten through life without hurting someone else—we Ladies most definitely included.

Alas, most apologies these days seem to be, "I'm sorry if you misinterpreted my words," followed by doubling down: "I don't care what ten thousand scientists say. I'm right, and no data will ever convince me I'm wrong, because I AM ALWAYS RIGHT." We as a society have this wrongful idea that if you admit a mistake, you somehow lose credibility.

Like you, we Ladies want a better world, in big ways and in small. Our podcast often discusses the devastating hurt caused by someone you considered a friend. How do you get past that? And what if YOU are the one who's wrong?

. . .

Kristan: *Once upon a time, my dearest son misbehaved in karate class. He was about five at the time, and the sensei made him sit outside. Dearest was crushed and embarrassed, because he loved Sensei Tom, and he hid his face against me and cried. I said to him, "Honey, we all make mistakes. It's what we do afterward that matters."*

That goes down as one of the top-three smart things I've said to my kids, but it applies to all of us. We all screw up. It's what we do afterward that matters, that defines our character, that creates our reputation, that lets us keep learning and growing as people. It's such a relief that I don't have to be right all the time, that I can screw up, learn from it and move on. Saying I'm sorry has never been a problem for me.

Joss: *I'm terrible at apologizing, because I'm a perfectionist. It's hard to be wrong when you spend so much time trying to be perfect. It means I've failed to anticipate everything, failed to ask for help, failed to keep all of those balls in the air, and, on top of that, I've hurt a friend. So I retreat a little bit to work up the nerve to apologize. I need to think for a while to make sure that I'm actually apologizing and not just excusing my behavior, because apologizing exposes you. It makes you feel vulnerable, and you have to overcome that feeling to offer a successful apology. The options are to never apologize or to give a bullshit excuse to save face—because it's too difficult to be wrong, to be vulnerable—but those options are unacceptable. You owe yourself and your friend much more than that.*

How soul-cleansing it can be to apologize and correct a misstep! How much lighter we would all feel if we knew we don't have to be perfect all the damn time! A *lot* lighter.

Being a thoughtful, responsible, empathetic person means that you will have to master the art of the apology. So what makes a good apology, both from the point of view of the person who delivers it and of the recipient? We're so glad you asked.

The Five Rs of Apologizing (and Examples of Crappy Attempts)

1. Recognition

Think about the hurt you have caused. Think about what it must have been like to be *the person you hurt* in that moment or situation. In today's society, we're essentially programmed to think about our own feelings first, which is why most of us fail when trying to apologize. We talk about how bad WE feel, not how bad we've made someone else feel. Remember, it's not about *your* feelings …it's about *her* feelings. Recognize that your behavior has caused someone else harm. Keep in mind that *not* recognizing the effect your behavior or words has had on your friend is the first step to offering a non-apology or fauxpology.

Crappy recognition: *I'm sorry that you think that I stole your idea during a meeting with the board of directors, but at least now we know that they totally support our efforts.* This kind of apology is the worst because it skillfully uses the word "sorry" while not being sorry at all.

Sincere recognition: *I am so sorry that I took credit for your idea. You must've felt so manipulated and upset.* (Sit back, maintain eye contact, and listen.)

2. Responsibility

Accept responsibility for what you did. Own it. You said what you said, and it was hurtful—or rude or insensitive or all of the above. Do *not* defend your actions. It's natural to recoil from the idea that you did something wrong, because it's embarrassing. But when you defend your actions—whether with *I'm having a bad time at work*, or *my cat died*, or *I'm getting a divorce*—you turn the conversation back to yourself and away from the one you hurt.

Do not **ever** tell the person if she had not done X, you would not have done Y. This move is called "blaming the victim." People who preface an apology with the notion that the other person's actions made them act badly are not apologizing. They're justifying their bad behavior. It's gaslighting. It's akin to an abusive man saying, "If you hadn't made me so mad, I wouldn't have beaten the shit out of you." Or "I only cheated on you because you ignored me."

If you really wish to make things right, you're going to have to admit fault. YOU are in control of what you do. No one else. NO ONE ELSE.

Crappy responsibility: *Last year, you invited Portia to go away with you on a weekend and not me, so I didn't feel like you'd want to come to my birthday bash, and that's why I didn't invite you.* This is tit-for-tat behavior. Petty. Adolescent. Bitchy. All about you. Not an apology. And she gets to have other friends. If that makes you want to exclude her, you're a crappy friend. YOU, Missy. Not her.

Sincere responsibility: *I'm sorry I didn't invite you to my birthday party. We've been friends for so long, and I should have remembered that and not been petty. Please forgive me.*

3. Remorse

Start by saying that you are very sorry. Even if you recognize the harm you did and take responsibility for it, your regret is meaningless without an apology. Imagine you had told a bride she looked ugly in her wedding dress. You later meet her, take responsibility for saying that hurtful thing ... but do not apologize. What that says then is that you're *not* sorry. Your "apology" is meaningless.

If instead you say something like, "Well, you DID look ugly, but I should not have said that out loud," you're a *really* crappy friend. People who behave this way are a little on the narcissistic side. They may acknowledge their actions, they know they hurt someone, but THEY AREN'T SORRY. There is no sincerity in "Sorry, not sorry."

Your apology doesn't have to be long-winded. There's nothing wrong with simply saying, "I'm very sorry, and I hope you'll forgive me."

If her response is, "Really? You're sorry? How are you sorry?" *then* you can offer up some of the ways you're taking responsibility for your actions. Explain that you've done a lot of soul-searching about why you did or said that hurtful thing, that you've found a good therapist, are reading some self-help books. Most important, explain that you'd sincerely like to be a better friend to her.

Stay away from the list of ways *you've* suffered, because, again, that would be making it all about you. Remember, your actions caused the problem. If now you feel bad and you're losing sleep or your health is affected, or if you got fired because of what you did, don't put that on her. The *last* thing you want is to make her somehow feel guilty or responsible because *you* fucked up.

Crappy remorse: *I'm so sorry I said you dress like a prostitute,* *even if you do. The minute the words left my mouth, I regretted them, and then the whole weekend was ruined for me. I couldn't sleep, and I started to say something a hundred times, but I just ended up crying in a closet, and I can't eat anything, and my therapist just dropped me, so I'm really floundering.*

Sincere remorse: *I had absolutely no right to tell you how to dress, and I'm very, very sorry. The truth is, you have a great sense of style, and I am really ashamed of what I said. Please forgive me.*

4. Reparation

Ask her if there's anything you can do to make up for your hurtful words or actions. Be willing to do what she asks, within reason. If she says, "Yes, you could disappear from the face of the earth," well, don't do that. But if she says, "I think it would be best if I didn't hear from you again," then you need to respect that.

It's your job to take it from there. If your friend says, "Nope. Can't think of anything. You take care now," ask her if she'd be willing to get together again sometime. Remember, we're talking about *friends* here. Maybe she misses you desperately and has been waiting for this apology. Don't assume she wants nothing to do with you. Let her set the tone. You do the work.

Crappy reparation: *I'm sorry I missed your mom's funeral. What a shitty friend I am! How can I make this up to you? Should I plow your driveway for a hundred years? Give you my firstborn?*

Sincere reparation: *You must be really stressed with settling your mom's estate, so I got you a gift certificate for a massage.*

5. Repetition:

There is also a bad R on this list: repetition. Repeating your crappy-friend behavior—it's the one thing that is guaranteed to make you lose your friend forever. It means you've learned nothing from your mistake. A friend shouldn't have to put up with bad behavior, especially if she's already asked you to cease and desist. They are more than welcome then to say, "I don't need you in my life." So be aware of your impact on people, good, bad and otherwise.

The Nitty Gritty of Apologies

Pick an appropriate time and venue.

In other words, be prepared so you can make your conversation a positive experience. Don't mutter "Sorry" as you walk past her desk at work. Don't apologize at her fiftieth-birthday bash, when she may want to have fun, or at her daughter's wedding, or when she's lying in a hospital bed. She has other things to think about. So make a date if you have to. Text her, email her, call her. Tell her "I'd like to talk to you about something if you have a little time."

Remember that this apology is FOR HER, not for you.

Of course, you'll get some benefit from it, too. However, the apology is not so much about clearing your conscience as it is about considering your friend and her feelings.

Depending on the egregiousness of your actions or

words, you may want to open right away with your apology. Look her in the eye and say, "I owe you an apology." Just saying these few words will start the discussion on the right note. You are making it clear that you feel you owe her something because you hurt her. Listen to the difference between "I need to apologize" or "I feel sick about what I did" vs. "I owe you an apology." The first statements are about *you*; the last one is about *her*. Make the apology all about her.

Be specific about what you said or did.

Being specific is part of taking ownership. Let's have none of this vague, "Hey, sorry things have been a little weird with us." Think of those wonderful twelve-step programs and how they work. One of those steps is, "Admit to our higher power, to ourselves, and to another human being the exact nature of our wrongs." This step has huge impact. You've thought a lot about what you did—now is the time for you to be really honest and admit it.

By taking ownership in your apology, you make yourself vulnerable, and you allow your friend to be vulnerable, too. She gets the chance to talk openly about the hurt you inflicted—and move past it to a better, stronger state of mind. *I didn't show up for your father's funeral at a time when you needed a friend more than ever.*

Talk about how your actions made HER feel.

Remember. This is not about you. It's about her. Otherwise, you're just asking her to take pity on you. "I am so embarrassed for what I said. I can't sleep. I've been agonizing over it, I'm binge-eating, and I'm just sick." On the surface, that may sound okay—but it's not. The focus is once again on YOU and your torment, not about her and her feelings.

You're asking her to feel bad about *your* pain after *you* inflicted pain on *her*. Not an apology.

Instead, how about something like this? *When I said we were all tired of hearing you whine about your mother, you must have felt shocked and upset and sucker-punched. I had no business making you feel awkward and upset. You should be able to expect sympathy and support from your friends, and I didn't give you that.*

One of our letters was from an author who behaved badly at a public event. She was in the audience, mean-tweeting and drinking. (Note: Twitter and booze do not pair well.) Her friend—who was on stage at the event—mentioned her favorite authors but did not include the letter writer. Feeling snubbed, Author-Behaving-Badly stormed out, knocking books off the table en route. She issued a vague apology on Twitter about her bad behavior but has never gotten over what she did—and neither has her friend, apparently, since they haven't spoken since.

We advised the badly behaved author to apologize specifically to her friend and to the other panelists at the event. Maybe something along the following lines: *I owe you an apology for behaving so badly at that book discussion two years ago. I stood up, interrupted you, and knocked your books off the table. That must have made you feel shocked and embarrassed, not to mention the fact that I completely derailed the discussion. That night was supposed to be about you and the other panelists, not about me and my issues. I am really sorry for the ridiculous interruption.*

If this were a different sort of situation—say your friend is battling a serious illness and you have been ignoring her and have never lifted a finger to help out—maybe you could start to do a few things for her now. Offer. Tell her you want to make amends, and while you know you can't erase what happened, you want to be a better friend. She might give you that chance. Or she might not. It's up to her.

The Benefits of a Good Apology

Your peace of mind: No matter what the outcome of your heartfelt, well-crafted apology, you put yourself out there. You acknowledged your mistake and tried to make amends. You've done some deep thinking and took responsibility, which is never a bad thing. That's how you grow. You don't have to lose sleep over your mistake anymore.

A more sincere and authentic friendship: You've humbled yourself and asked for forgiveness. She heard you. That shit matters. Now you can move forward.

Self-respect: What you did to cause the hurt was wrong, but what you did afterward is important to acknowledge. As Kristan told her boy, "Everyone makes mistakes. It's what we do afterward that matters." It is hard to admit that you were wrong, but you did it anyway. Even if it doesn't get you the friend back, you behaved like a respectful, mindful adult.

Respect from others: Maybe your friend will immediately forgive you, and all will be well again. She'll probably respect you more now, because you took responsibility for your behavior. If others are involved, they too will see that she forgave and views the friendship as something worth continuing. If she decides she *doesn't* want to be friends with you anymore, word may still spread that you owned up. Karma will reward you.

Personal growth: Once, you were a person who said and did stupid stuff. Now, after this experience, you're trying much harder not to. You have an opportunity next time to be more mature, more thoughtful, and a better friend.

Apologies take courage and character. Someone who can admit a mistake and apologize for it isn't weak at all. She's strong, insightful and considerate. Be those things.

CHAPTER 12

ENDING A FRIENDSHIP

YOU'VE HAD THAT NIGGLING FEELING FOREVER NOW. Do you really like this person? Are you phoning it in? If you met her today, would you want to spend time with her?

Take time to really analyze what, in your eyes, makes a friend the absolute best. Use the most caring, healthy, trusting relationship you have as your guide. It doesn't matter if it's your relationship with your dad, your sister or your husband that has set the bar high. Be specific in how you answer these questions, because they will help you assess what type of friend you're dealing with—a work friend, a fun acquaintance, or someone who will stand beside you, always with your best interests front and center.

- Has your friendship withstood the test of time?
- Have you been through tough situations in the past and been helped and nurtured by your friend?
- In what ways did the two of you build trust over time?
- When and where and how were boundaries

established? Did you cross any of them? Did your
friend? Was that situation resolved? How?
- Are you able to communicate your feelings
comfortably?
- What happens when you disagree?
- How does your friend treat the other people in
her life? How do you treat yours?

You've thought and thought about this, discussed it with
your therapist, woken up at night because finally, you know.

The time has come to end the friendship.

For whatever reasons, it's over, or it's about to be. And
that's okay. Once upon a time, you were friends, and there
were reasons for this friendship. History. Common interests.
Kids the same age. Same neighborhood. Shared profession.
Knitting circle. The Michael B. Jordan Fan Club. But you are
not obliged to continue dealing with a person who isn't
adding to your life any longer.

You don't need grounds to divorce a friend ...but,
because we are women, we often feel like we have to justify
our actions. So if you feel you need to do that, here are some
legitimate friendship-enders.

Serious betrayal. There's no coming back from that. She
slept with your husband? Deliberately damaged your career?
Lied about you? She's not your friend, and you know it. In
the case of a heinous breach of trust, we Ladies recommend a
swift guillotine approach: "We're done. I'm blocking your
number and your social media accounts. Don't contact me."

Separate ways. That old saying, "Friends for a reason, friends
for a season" has merit. You might've been besties when you
were both in medical school, but now you're head of ortho-
pedic surgery, and she only does surgery on pinkie toes.

Without the commonalities of your long-ago shared experience, it might just be that the friendship has run its course. It doesn't mean you don't like each other anymore. It's just that the foundation of the friendship is no longer intact. It's okay. You'll always be fond of her ...but your time together has come to an end.

Endless conflicts. She nitpicks everything you say. There's a current of tension in the air every time you get together. You argue—and not in a good-natured or intelligent way. You argue in ways that say, "I'm right and you're wrong, and you're stupid if you don't see that." This relationship is not a friendship. It is a form of self-induced torture.

She's an energy suck:. You feel exhausted at the thought of seeing her and drained when you get home afterward. Maybe she just takes up all the air, holding forth, wanting your admiration, awe and praise. Listen, we all know that person, and it's not your job to be her audience, nodding and applauding. Or—also on this spectrum—maybe your friend is needy, always in crisis, always taking so much more than she gives. It's okay if you just run out of steam. Again, it's not up to you to fix her—and even if you wanted to, you couldn't.

She makes you feel bad about yourself. One of our listeners wrote to us about her fear that her friend constantly judges her and finds her lacking. Another listener wrote about her friend's newfound sense of superiority and entitlement after getting a high-paying job. Making you feel bad is not what friends are for. In fact, that is the opposite of what friends are for. Your nasty grandmother can make you feel like crap because she's your grandmother, but friends ...you choose your friends. If you need your snuggle blanket and a visit to your therapist after you spend time with your friend, reconsider how you're spending your time.

You just don't like or respect her anymore. Sure, she was fun and hosted great parties and was always up for having coffee or hanging out. But when she outed herself as a racist or homophobe and defended her jokes about "those people," you knew it was time to leave.

Whatever the reason, you know and accept that it's time to end the friendship. Even so, you may well have a lot of strong feelings about this: Nostalgia for the good times. Bitterness for the time wasted on a friend who didn't deserve it. Sadness that you're going to hurt someone. Loss (she might've been a bitch, but she was always free for a late-night run to Wendy's). A sense of triumph that you're finally going to amputate this gangrenous limb from your body. Fear, because you hate confronting anyone. Glee, maybe, because this former friend really hurt you and now you're going to let her have it, big time.

Let's stop a minute. We women are a complicated lot. We make Siggy Freud look like a six-year-old Cub Scout when it comes to examining feelings. We're capable of hating and loving someone in the same second. We might be muttering "piss off, bitch" under our breath, but we would give her a kidney if she needed one.

These emotions are normal. We'll all feel them someday to some degree—and probably already have. Maybe we're experiencing them right now. We're women. This is what we do—we roll around in the "feels."

And yet, you're doing yourself a disservice if you give your time to a person who brings nothing good to your life. By continuing to stay in a crappy friendship, you might feel magnanimous, giving her your time, including her in events, texting her to say hi …but the truth is, if you actively dislike her, your fake friendship and affection is a *de facto* lie.

So, time to go.

How to Break Up, Without, You Know…the Drama

The Slow Fade: The Slow Fade is indirect and designed to keep you from facing unpleasantries. The Slow Fade is built upon the idea that your friend will get the hint—that you're just not that into her anymore.

Your friend Dolly contacts you. Your Slow Fade starts by waiting to respond to her texts, DMs, phone calls, invitations. Rather than instantly answering, you let the message linger awhile, indicating that it's not high on your priority list. Then you answer politely. *Sounds fun but I'm busy that night. Have a great time!* Or *Sorry I couldn't answer right away. Work's been crazy.*

Maybe Dolly asks for your advice. Don't give it, even if you're tempted. As she is telling you her story, remember Dr. Khaleesi's line—"That sounds hard. What's your plan?" In this way, you're marking a clear division between you and her, and yet you can't be blamed for being callous. Resist the urge to solve her problems or serve as her authority figure.

Another strategy in the Slow Fade is to mention other social commitments without offering an alternate time to get together. *Sorry, I'm going away with some friends from work that weekend.* Or *I have a date that night.* Or *I'm volunteering at the community center this weekend. Thanks for asking, though!* Or *Oh, gosh, I already made plans.* (Note: an evening sitting in your chair with your dog, reading and eating popcorn totally counts as "plans.")

Don't lie, though. "I'm sick" might turn into Dolly bringing you soup and finding you surrounded by your book club, of which she is not a member. Lies are hard to keep track of, and they chip away at one's soul. And, inevitably, you'll get caught.

If you *have* to see Dolly from time to time—maybe you live in the same neighborhood or work together—be pleasant, friendly and unavailable. A wave, "Pretty shirt!" and on you go on with your business.

Hopefully, Dolly will see the pattern and get the message. But based on our experience and on the many letters we receive from our listeners, Dolly may not see anything... which brings us to the next approach.

Hinting: For those of us who go out of their way to avoid hurting a person's feelings, the next stop on the breakup train is hinting. *My New Year's resolution is to surround myself with positive people.* Will Dolly understand that she's not one of those people? Uh ...maybe. To make the point clearer, you could say, "I'm spending more time on self-care," implying that this is a solo endeavor. If Dolly doesn't pick up on the broad hints, you may need to turn to the next, and most brutal way, to end the friendship.

Ghosting: In most cases, we Ladies don't recommend ghosting—the complete and sudden erasure of another person in every way possible without any explanation. You block her from your phone, your social media, you don't return calls or letters. You essentially pretend she doesn't exist.

The only times this approach might be advisable is when the friend you're ghosting has caused you real psychological or physical damage, to the point that any additional contact would cause you more harm. Ghosting is for those times when an incredibly important line has been crossed, and there's no going back.

But we Ladies hope things never get this far. Ghosting is an extreme statement that your former friend is not worth even a text. It's dramatic, and it offers no answers and no sense of closure. Most people don't deserve that harsh treatment—and it doesn't make *you* feel good, either. Which brings us to the best method of all: an actual conversation.

One Honest Conversation: Yes. Kristan's special unicorn in the friendship world. In the case of breaking up, you go face to face, live and in person, and tell her you don't wish to be friends any more. (We know. We broke out in hives just typing that sentence.) That seems so cruel. You don't want to hurt feelings! But are we bad people for just …telling the truth? Maybe you're one of those people who has no problem just spitting it out, and if so, good for you! For a lot of us, it's hives…but just because something is hard doesn't mean it's not the right thing to do.

How to Have the Honest Conversation

Plan ahead.

Step one is to think about your end goal. Don't just react to Dolly's latest infraction. Blurting out what you want to say, either in person or in an email, text or IM, rarely has the desired results and tends to create more drama than is needed.

Your goal is to end this friendship as kindly, clearly and efficiently as you can. You might be tempted to bring up every negative interaction you've ever had as proof that you're justified in your actions. Don't do this. A debate is not your goal. This honest conversation is so you can amputate the friendship in a clean, decisive way, and the healing can begin. Because you *will* need to heal, and so will she.

Set your tone.

If you're writing a letter, text or email, remember that it's easy to misinterpret tone in someone's writing. Do your best to let her know what yours is. *This is going to be tough to read, but please know that I'm trying to be honest and kind.* Don't be angry. Be firm. Just as with a person you don't want to date anymore, don't string the person along. You don't want to be friends anymore You're allowed to choose that.

Be brief.

Even if you have a list a mile long of excellent examples of how she hurt/ignored/belittled/dismissed you, remember your goal: you want to end this, not perpetuate the discussion.

If you feel you must address a specific situation—as in, she got drunk, once again, but this time at your wedding, and vomited on your mother—focus on how it made you feel, rather than what she did. *Dolly, when you got trashed at my wedding, it felt disrespectful and attention-seeking. When you vomited on my mom, I was horrified. That was not something I wanted to deal with on my wedding day. I want a friend who's able to behave appropriately, especially on a day that was so important to me. That was the final straw, and I'm really sorry, but I just don't want to keep working at this friendship.*

Be honest.

Tell her that you simply can't give her the kind of

friendship she seems to need. Does she expect you to respond to each text within thirty seconds? Does she get resentful if you have other plans? Does she let months pass without reaching out? *I think we have different expectations of what friendship means.* It's a situation most women encounter at some point in their lives, and it's perfectly fine to address it.

Thank her for the good times and wish her the best.

There *were* good times. There's a reason you've been putting up with this friend as long as you have, even as you recognized that the relationship was deteriorating and became riddled with problems. You don't hate this person. You just don't want her in your life anymore. Acknowledge the good times and say good-bye.

Prepare yourself for her response, as well as possible fallout.

Her responses may include angry Facebook postings, furious or tearful letters, phone calls at 3 a.m., fifty texts in one hour—or maybe just one rude but very clear gesture. There's a good chance she'll tell your mutual acquaintances how rotten, cruel, insensitive and unkind you are.

Remember three things.

Her feelings are hurt. She's probably going to react in some way. Unfortunately, not many friendships end with the words, "Hey, that's fine. I feel the same way. Take good care!"

No one can hurt your reputation except you. If Dolly calls everyone you know and says, "She was so *mean!* I'm so *hurt!*" well, they know you, and they know her. Maybe there will be a pile-on against you. Maybe there will be a pile-on in support of you. Either way, you stay classy, kid.

You're done. You don't have to tell every friend you had that you *finally* got rid of Dolly, and you said this, then that, and your hands were shaking, but you did it, and she cried, and it was awful. There's no need for this. You're done. You did the hard thing. You did it as kindly as you could, and it's OVER.

Take time to reflect.

You might be quite sad, you might feel victorious, you may feel angry or all of those things in turn or at once. If this person was once a cherished pal, you'll miss her. That's normal. Grieve what used to be, or even what you *thought* used to be.

We've all had that friend we truly loved at first, but not all friendships are meant to last forever. It doesn't mean we won't miss the olden days. It doesn't mean those weekends spent together weren't really, really fun. It just means you're a little older and wiser now. It means that if you met her today, knowing what you now know, you might not make the same choices. It means that you're going to invest your time in other areas, and you get to do that. The more honestly you deal with these feelings, the faster you'll get past this breakup and move into a better, cleaner head space and uncluttered heart.

CHAPTER 13

GETTING DUMPED

SOMETIMES YOU MAY NOT BE THE ONE ENDING THE friendship. Sometimes, you're the one on the receiving end.

One of the worst things about being dumped by someone we consider a friend is the shock. We Ladies have both experienced this "punched in the face" feeling. You feel hot and ashamed. Your eyes fill. You want to defend yourself. You say, "But …but . . .but" a few times. You can't *believe* this is happening. What did you DO to deserve this? Were you so horrible in some way you didn't realize? You're scared. What will life be like without this friend? You're embarrassed. Someone found you so lacking that they don't want to see or talk to you anymore.

Yes, it's horrible. We are so, so sorry. But when the shock subsides, you might see a few things more clearly.

The friendship had been withering for a while. When you have some distance and can you look closely, you realize that this friendship hasn't really been that great lately. It became harder and harder to get together, and when you did the conversations weren't the same. The friendship had become more of a habit, and nothing else.

She was not the person you thought you knew...or vice versa. Most of us make this mistake at least once. Your hopes for the friendship, or your shared history, the good qualities you both have—these can all blind you to certain realities. It may take some time to see that, given the shock you've just been dealt, but think on it. Maybe you had the Insta-Friend connection and made all sorts of happy assumptions about your new friend, and she about you. Now that time has passed, you may see that you simply weren't a good fit.

You made mistakes. Yes, you. You missed her thirtieth birthday party, got trashed at her wedding and vomited on her mother. You made snide comments about her job, her house, her wife. You took her for granted. Maybe that mattered to her more than you knew. Maybe you were too much of a Negative Nancy or talked only about yourself 90 percent of the time. Reflect on your own role in the friendship. Here's an opportunity for self-growth.

We Ladies are fully behind the idea of owning your mistakes. It may be too late now to save the relationship, but this can be a pivotal moment for you. Imagine being able to write to her and say, "You're right. I wasn't a great friend, and I apologize for taking you for granted. I respect your decision and wish you the best, and who knows? Maybe someday we'll reconnect. I appreciate all the good times we had together."

You may never know her reasons. Maybe you were a *great* friend, and so was she! You honestly have no idea why she is dumping you. You don't have to solve the mystery, and even if you want to, you may fail. Chances are good that she's not secretly dying of a rare disease and can't bear to put you through the loss of a friend. Hon, she dumped you. You don't know why. You had no indication that she was unhappy or bored or a sociopath—not one, but here you are, dumped. It happens.

For whatever reason, you were no longer valuable *to her*. Remember this: That doesn't mean you're not valuable as a human. You are. And you *will* have other friends. Trust us.

How to Get Over It

Whether you were dumper or the dumpee, you've suffered a significant loss—or you wouldn't be reading this section. This friend was once precious to you. You enjoyed her company, confided in her, laughed with her. What you had was real to you, and the relationship may have lasted decades.

Now you feel like your heart has been torn out of your chest. This is, sadly, normal. You're grieving. You're in mourning. The experience of losing a friend can be worse than a divorce, as one of our listeners wrote. As women, we believe in being friends as soulmates. And sometimes, that happens. But not always.

Healing. It's going to take a while. How long it will take varies but give yourself permission to feel like shit—for a while. Cry, go to a kick-boxing class, burn the box of stuff she gave you, eat a bag of Bugles and watch crappy TV shows all weekend. And then …well, we Ladies have some suggestions about what to do next.

. . .

Call your therapist. If you don't have a therapist, get one. Seriously. Women thrive on friendship. It's an absolutely essential, vital part of most women's lives, and the loss of one can have huge ramifications, including depression, inability to trust, loneliness, even physical effects like fatigue or hormones going crazy. Dealing with these tough feelings is difficult. Your life is going to look different without her. Help is available. Get it.

Remind yourself that this friendship ended for a reason. One of you wasn't getting what she needed from it. Whether you broke it off or she did, the friendship wasn't healthy, even if you didn't know that until it was too late. Otherwise, you would've stayed friends. It's as simple and painful as that.

If you did something that caused the friendship to end—something crappy—apologize, own it and let her go. Be an adult. Say, *What I said was ignorant and hurtful, and I'm really sorry* Or *You're right. I gossiped about you, and I'm sorry.* These types of statements will let you move on with the knowledge that you *are* trying to do and be better.

Do stuff. Go to the gym, take a class, see what's happening in your area that might interest you. Get out of the house, missy. While you're still in mourning, recognize that the absence of this friend has made space in your life for other things. Consider volunteering, because doing something for others is a surefire way to feel better about yourself. Maybe your grandma needs her attic cleaned out. Maybe the mom down the street could use some free babysitting. The animal shelter needs help. Get out there and do some good in this world.

Stop stalking your former friend. Oh, please, of course you are. *We* each have, and so we know it ain't gonna help. Neither is rereading all your texts and emails. The friendship is *over*. Delete. Purge. Give away the earrings she gave you. Buy new earrings.

Resist the urge to prove you're the better person by campaigning against her. Don't vague-book—those mysterious posts about the betrayal of trust, or "just when you thought you knew someone," or "ouch, that knife in my back." You are not in a courtroom trying to sway jurors to your side. You are having a human experience. You have nothing to prove. People can and will make their own judgments. Live your life with integrity, and all will be well.

Do not drink and dial/text/Facebook/Tweet/Snapchat/Instagram/TikTok, etc. Sobriety is your friend post breakup. Grief and alcohol don't mix, and you will likely do or say something you will regret. Every day without contact with and attention to this friend is a step in the right direction. Alcohol and other substances lower your inhibitions and tell you not only that you're a fabulous dancer, calling her at 3 a.m. and telling her off is what you *need*. Don't listen. Go for a walk instead.

Get your post-breakup scripts ready. You may well have mutual friends or workmates who will ask, "Hey, what's going on with you and Quinoa?" If you have a line or two at hand, you'll be less likely to burst into tears. Your script should not be, "Quinoa is a right bitch and she DUMPED ME, can you believe it, after I sat by her mother's hospital bed and fed her parrot when she was on vacation?" No. Your script should be something like, "We're not as close as we used to be" or "We don't have as much in common now that our kids are grown" or "I haven't seen her for a while." Try to avoid sowing seeds of gossip. Don't air your dirty laundry to anyone with ears. We're all about staying classy here.

Likewise, be prepared to run into her again, and have that script ready, too. Do not lurch to a halt when you spot her and start crying, pointing or accusing. Do not hide (although the temptation may be *really* strong to do this). Don't pretend you don't see her. Don't pretend you're still besties. Be civil. *Hi, Quinoa, how have you been? How's your mom? Give her my best.* And then . . .onward. Keep those feet moving forward.

Start meeting new people. Volunteer, as we suggested earlier. Go to MeetUp and see if there's a hike or foreign film this weekend. Go slowly and carefully. Your heart is still sore. Take what you've learned from the friendship that broke and use those things in crafting a new friendship. It won't be the same...and it may well be better.

Vet new friends carefully. However the friendship ended, it is a significant experience that brings up a range of powerful emotions, so take your time forming new friendships.

. . .

Start small. Joining a group can be a great way to see what kind of a person someone is, because you'll get to see how she interacts with others before you make an emotional investment.

Share your personal information slowly. Don't blurt out your life story during your first coffee date. See what circumstances you have in common—*I went to school in California, too!*—before talking about heartbreak, loss and love.

Watch for red flags. And pay attention to what they're telling you. You don't want to glance in the rearview mirror of life and see the road littered with the bodies of ex-best friends because you didn't pay attention.

Take your time. Remember that only time will tell. Insta-Friendships are fraught with dangers, though hitting it off right away with someone certainly isn't a bad thing. Just be aware of what you *think* and what you *know*. You can only really know someone over time.

Take care of yourself. Losing a friend can be as significant and painful as losing a partner, parent or sibling. Know that you're not alone. Lean on the other people in your life and take good care of yourself. You're gonna be okay.

CHAPTER 14

CRAP-FREE FRIENDSHIPS

THOSE WHO WANT GOOD THINGS FOR THEIR FRIENDS
for their sake are most truly friends; for they do this by
reason of their own nature and not coincidentally; therefore
their friendship lasts as long as they are good—and virtue is
an enduring thing.

—Aristotle, "Nicomachean Ethics" (340 BC)

In other words, be a good person and you'll be a good friend.

That Aristotle really knew his shit.

But how do we "be good" in these supremely odd and
ever-changing times? What does it mean to be a good friend,
when facing curated social media feeds, missed and misunderstood electronic communications, and unexpected life
events? What makes you a good friend—the kind of friend
that is draped in green flags instead of red ones?

Green Flag # 1: Compassion

We Ladies know it takes work to be a good person—compassionate, considerate and all the other good and kind things. We all have so much baggage, trunks and suitcases and carryons full. The point is, in order to be a friend draped in *green* flags, you need to be self-aware. But first you need to recognize that you *have* bullshit and need to work on it. You also need to recognize that not only do you have bullshit but so do other people—even that friend of yours.

In other words, be compassionate. We are all generally programmed to think about how *we* feel about something before we think about how others feel. You had a movie night planned with your bestie, and she canceled at the last minute. Your first thought is for yourself. *Damn. I was really looking forward to that, and now I'm bummed.* We Ladies are not suggesting that you change that way of thinking entirely—we are only suggesting that your very next reasonable thought should be how that something might be affecting your friend. *It's unlike Kristan to cancel, especially for a Michael B. Jordan movie. I wonder what's going on.*

This may be incredibly difficult to do when a major life event—like a new baby or a death or the endless draining work of being a caretaker—is the something looming over you. But a real friend will make it easy. She'll offer to help. She'll be there. She will put herself in your shoes and think about what she might need if she were in your position. You don't have to feel pressure to go to the movies or have a girl's night, but you *can* communicate with her, even if it's just to let her know that you're overwhelmed and may be off the grid for a while.

Don't assume that your friend can read your mind. Should she know? Maybe. Does she also have her own shit going on? Probably. Notice the order of thoughts: I've got my own crap going on, but so does my bestie.

On the flip side, if your friend is going through major life changes, employ as much compassion as you possibly can. For example, don't take her silence or distance personally. It hurts when you haven't heard from her in days/weeks, even though you've left voicemails, emailed, DM-ed. We get it. If you view the situation with an abundance of compassion, instead of feeling hurt by her silence, you're able separate her behavior from your *interpretation* of her behavior.

We Ladies know it's hard to keep from analyzing your friend's behavior (especially when the behavior is unfamiliar), either alone or over cocktails with another friend or a group of friends. So, here are a few tricks to help you slow your roll, i.e., not jump to conclusions:

Meditate and/or practice deep breathing. Meditation has been proven to lower stress and improve focus, but it can also calm the nonstop chatter of your brain that keeps you from relaxing and sleeping.

Take a break. Go for a walk or go to the gym, listen to music, get a massage, cook something delicious (yes, eating macaroni and cheese can actually make you a better friend.) Do something that activates the five senses and makes you more aware of your environment and your place in it. The experience will put some distance between you and the insecure feelings that could (unnecessarily) turn your friend's actions into a dagger through your heart.

Take care of yourself. Eat healthy (okay, so not macaroni and cheese all the time). Hydrate…with water. Remember, wine doesn't make you smarter, only more willing to drink and dial, or text. Get in the habit of being positive—*Oh,* *what a pretty day!*—grateful and calm. It builds resilience and peace. Get at least eight hours of sleep each night. It sounds like an obvious thing, but getting a good night's rest promotes focus and keeps your intellectual and physiological functions humming like a well-oiled machine.

Find opportunities to be selfless. Helping someone else in big ways or in small tends to put things in perspective. Whether you're organizing your friend's closet (at her request, obviously) or helping out at the animal shelter, or spending an hour on the phone with someone who's going through a rough time, you're making sure you're doing your part and being kind.

Becoming a more compassionate person doesn't happen by magic and doesn't happen overnight. It's a conscious activity, like remembering to go to the gym and then actually *going*. The seeds you sow by being a more compassionate person will yield immediate positive results for you and positive long-term results for your friendship.

Green Flag #2: Respect

When a friendship is new and still developing, it's easy to read and respect the other person's boundary cues. Getting to know your new friend's likes and dislikes, her quirks and cocktail preferences become priorities as you build your relationship. During these initial moments, don't make assumptions. Having common interests is important, but just because you like to craft and she likes to craft doesn't mean that you'll be best friends forever. Take your time. Begin as you mean to go on by being honest and communicative. Listen first, respond second...and remember her answers. *She said she took the job for the experience, but the pay was shit. I'll invite her to dinner at my place rather than pick a swanky restaurant.* The boundaries you both set early on will lay the foundation of a healthy relationship.

When your friendship has aged like a fine wine, it may be harder to establish boundaries. There is a lot of history and familiarity. After all, you were the one back in the day who stood guard at the bathroom-stall door at the club while she frolicked with the hot guy from the bar. In fact, the many flings you saw her through could earn you a tattoo on your forehead. Now, all of a sudden, she wants you to respect her "relationship" with her latest "love."

Maybe you know how this new fling is going to end, and you'd much rather skip the awkward brunch and head straight for the post-mortem cocktails, but you respect the boundary. Now more than ever is the time to avoid the kind of familiarity that breeds contempt. Now is the time to respect that your friend knows what she's about and can handle whatever's coming. Even if you end up being right, be the person who gives your friend space to succeed or fail at her own pace.

Respect for your friend should grow as your friendship grows. If you find yourself unable to respect a new and sudden boundary—*Don't call me after 7 p.m., ever*— take the time to evaluate the reasons for your resistance. Are you uncomfortable because this new boundary is genuinely detrimental to your friend (like, her boo is really controlling and you fear he's cutting her off from friends)…or because it inconveniences you, conflicts with your preconceived notions about your friend and interferes with the established routines of your friendship?

When Kristan is on vacation with her family, Joss knows not to call. Not because Kristan wouldn't take the call, but because she would, and Joss respects Kristan's devotion to family time. Rather than put her in the position of spending two hours on the phone, Joss will wait till she comes back. But she also knows that if she were in the hospital, clutching her chest, Kristan would move heaven and earth to be there for her.

Green Flag #3: Honest communication

What's weird about communication is that it's not just about being honest. It's about being *vulnerable*, which is so much harder. Being honest with your friend, telling her that those ripped jeans that she thinks are so fabulous are really not is way easier than revealing your deepest secrets and wounds. Vulnerability creates intimacy, which strengthens the bonds of friendship. Vulnerability strengthens any relationship bond, actually, so make sure honest communication is a frequently used tool in your toolbox.

Be honest but temper honesty with compassion. Lately, we Ladies have received letters from listeners about "honesty" that's just plain mean. Jokes that are pointed and oftentimes cutting are tossed around with an "omg, jk," or "I'm just an honest person. I can't change who I am." These and similar gaslight-y phrases are red flags and do not reflect the type of honest communication we encourage. Real honesty is fueled by good intentions, and the previous examples are fueled by selfishness. A friend's intention should be to help her friend.

If you're the one who's not being honest, ask yourself why. The answer is usually rooted in fear and/or shame. Even telling tiny, white lies may be exposing a wound that's holding you back. For example, like Joss, you may say yes to a lot of invitations, knowing that you're a major introvert and generally like people's dogs better than you like people. When the time comes to go to an event, you may frantically think of excuses. *Oh no! I've been hit by a bus and can't come to dinner!* (And then my friend Kristan would say to me, *Is that your introversion talking?* [kind honesty] *Never fear, I've made you a lovely cocktail that will cure any bus-related injuries* [followed up by action]. *Please remember to tie up the back of your hospital gown when you come over* [further acknowledgment and acceptance of my bullshit.]

Why even say yes to these invitations in the first place, you ask? Take your pick: maybe you don't want to hurt people's feelings, you want people to like you, you don't want to disappoint folks who want to spend time with you. Or maybe you've legitimately forgotten about the event and now that it's time to go, you'd rather have a Netflix-and-popcorn night.

But acknowledging that your social anxiety stems from the fear that no one is going to talk to you because you grew up being told you were rude and horrible…that takes vulnerability and trust. That's the kind of honesty that deepens a friendship. Not that you get out of every invitation every time…but at least your friend understands where your hesitation comes from.

Of course, the easiest way to handle the situation is to not accept so many invitations in the first place or maybe get a better handle on your calendar. It's a bit harder is to confront your fear, dismantle it, and then, with kindness, tell the truth and follow up with action, to reinforce sincerity. *I'm so sorry, my calendar got away from me and I won't be able to attend, but I feel like we haven't talked in ages. Can I interest you in a phone chat after dinner tonight?*

Green Flag #4: Trust

Trust is so tricky. It takes forever to build and can be lost either slowly by degrees or in the blink of an eye. There are two things you can do to safeguard and nurture it, so that if bad times do hit, you will have solid ground to stand on:

1. Do what you say you're going to do.
2. Be where you say you're going to be.

Being reliable is not nearly as sexy as being mysterious and spontaneous, but when you're going through the wringer, who is more helpful—the friend who's always on time or the friend who's unpredictable? Be reliable to establish your friend's trust at the outset and look for signs of reliability in your friend. Building a trusting relationship takes time. The Insta-Friendships we write about in Chapter 3 are oftentimes all smoke, flash and mirrors. Real relationships are like lotus flowers: beautiful as they float on the pond but with deep roots that reach through dark waters to anchor that beauty.

Green Flag #5: Openness

Finally, stay open to growth and change. Be as wholly and authentically *you* as you can be. Figure out your default settings—be okay with what's working but be proactive about changing what's not. Then show your friend the same courtesy, because friendship can't work without reciprocation. As you grow, learn new things and evolve, so too does your friend. Stay open to change, which happens in all relationships. That sullen teenager who hated shopping with you? She loves it now. Go figure. Your partner, who hated all things outdoors, suddenly decides to start hiking? That could be a good thing. A great thing, even.

Sometimes the inability to accept something new limits the growth of a friendship. Misunderstanding thrives when familiar pathways veer into unexpected territory. Your buddy has liked chocolate mint ice cream for the twenty-five years that you've known her, eschewing all other flavors with a sneer that you can do a pretty good imitation of. All of a sudden, as of yesterday, she's team peach pie all the way. Seems like a small thing, but it's potentially the first of a thousand small twists that can turn you from besties into feeling like strangers.

The idea of "best friends forever" makes the same assumptions that the romantic "happily ever after" does: okay, we've achieved this milestone and now we're done, happy, perfect. The truth is that every relationship—especially the one we have with ourselves—is dynamic, fluid. Good things come from acknowledging this phenomenon, including shared trust, increased intimacy, and honest communication.

Authenticity is the secret sauce, you guys. Knowing who you are helps you find your inner circle. It helps you to understand and chart the course of your friendships. It helps you see the red flags from a mile away and it helps you to recover from loss. We Ladies hope you will prioritize the process of self-discovery. Learn who you are and what you're made of. You'll be a better friend, and person, for it. Be true to yourself, be true to your friends and happiness is sure to follow.

We wish you a lifetime of friendships—old and new—of the highest quality, the deepest trust and the best of times.

—Kristan and Joss

ABOUT THE AUTHORS

Kristan Higgins is the New York Times & USA TODAY bestselling author of many novels and spends her days dissecting personalities, both for her job and in real life.

Joss Dey is the USA TODAY bestselling author of Undertow, and is fascinated with toxic friendships, how they develop, and why we suffer through them.

For more information on Crappy Friends, visit www.crappyfriends.net. You can find Kristan at www.kristanhiggins.com and Joss at www.jossdey.com.

Made in the USA
Coppell, TX
04 January 2021